AF589586

Published 2021

Cover and book design by Buzzy Lewis
Photos sourced from pexels.com

Printed in Australia by IngramSpark
Edited by Kevin Miller (www.kevinmillerxi.com)

Library of Congress Cataloging-in-Publication Data is available from the National Library of Australia

Printed book: ISBN 978-0-6452519-0-6

Author: Bethany (Buzzy) Lewis
Title: Being Creative

Failurefriendly.com
@failure_friendly

All Inquiries: Buzzy Lewis, buzzy@failurefriendly.com

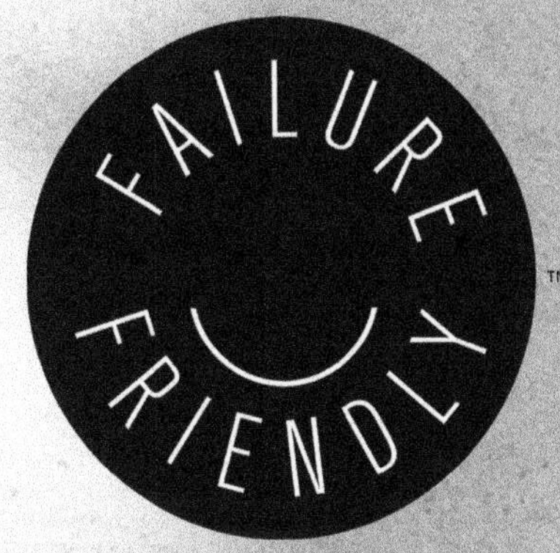

written on Gunditjmara country.

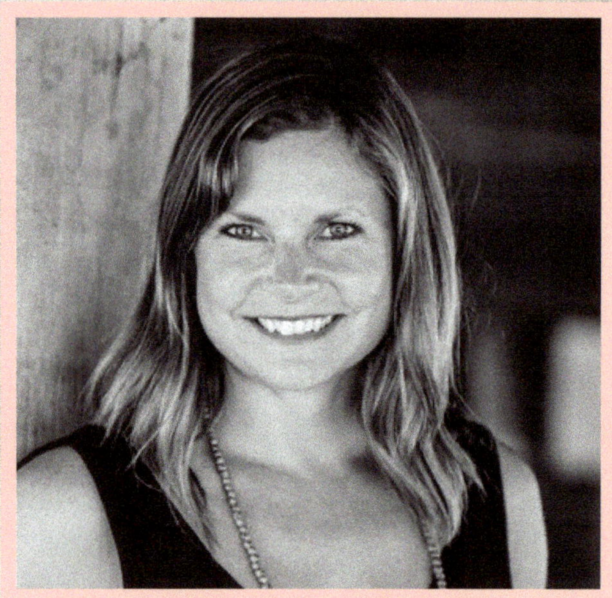

Nikki Smith is a registered psychologist who works as a career change coach.

She helps corporate clients, teachers, journalists and more to uncover their dream role: a role that plays to their unique strengths, purpose and lifestyle needs. One that gives them more meaning and freedom. She then helps them to make it a reality.

Nikki has changed careers three times herself from event manager, to musician to psychologist.

She interviews her clients about their career changes on her podcast which you can access via her website www.nikkismithcoach.com

NIKKI'S FOREWORD

When Buzzy was a newly graduated graphic designer, she felt such intense worry and resistance with her first client that she procrastinated and hid. The client stopped calling.

It's so easy to let our thoughts prevent us from showing up as fully as we can as a creative human being. Our thoughts are stories, not facts, yet we can believe them fiercely and allow them to shape our reality.

Are you a perfectionist?

Do you have ideas and procrastinate spectacularly?

Do you have bold dreams and continue to play small?

When someone starts to re-discover their creativity (yes, we are all creative but may not yet know it) there are so many potential pitfalls that can slow them down, make them doubt yourself and get them stuck.

Buzzy writes about her experience of re-discovering her creativity and gives you a road-map to recognise and potentially avoid those pitfalls that took her years to unpack and figure out.

She shares practical insights and advice based on what she has learnt from six years exploring her own fear of failure.

No matter what stage you're at on your creative journey, you will gain from this.

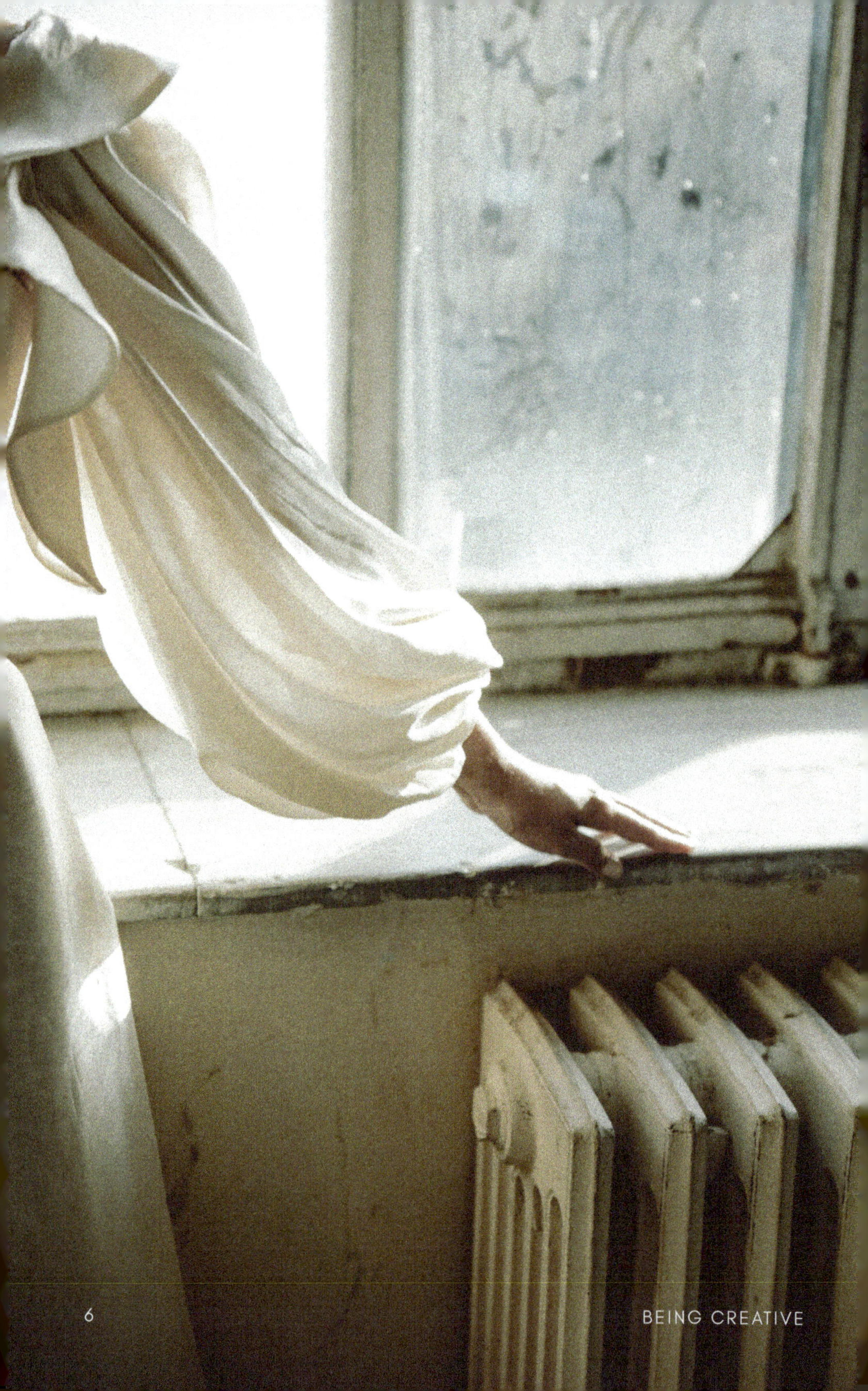

DO YOU CONSENT?

Before you read a single word of the advice that is loaded into this book, I want to ask for your permission. Are you open to me sharing with you what I've learnt about the fear of failure and creativity?

Unsolicited advice, no matter how well intentioned, is shame in disguise. If someone takes it upon themselves to advise us, it indicates there is something wrong with us that needs improving or correcting. It subtly implies that solutions lay outside of ourselves, and that someone else knows us and our needs better than we do.

At first glance this book may look like a prescriptive step-by-step guide or one-size-fits-all approach. Walk the steps if they feel true to you. However there is a deeper message to be found beyond these steps. Within the journey that evolves in each chapter of this book, is something I invite you to discover for yourself.

1. FRAMEWORK

Create a safe space

p.19-27

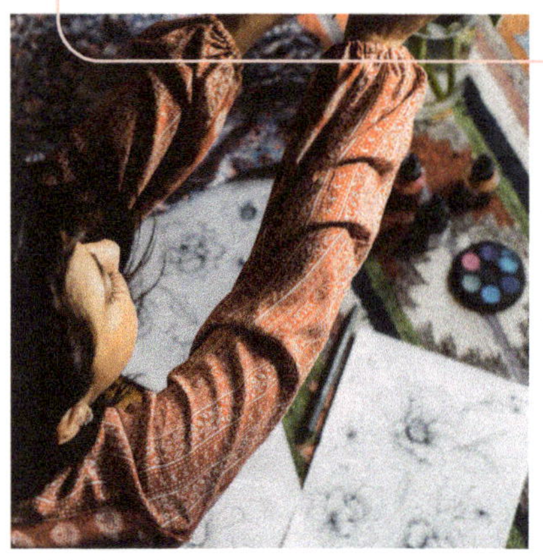

2. SKILL SET

Learn the skills needed to clear the blocks

p.29-39

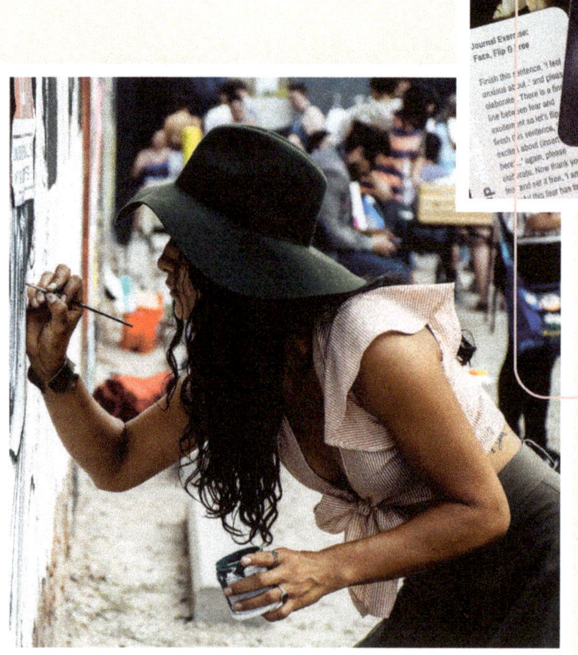

3. PRACTICE

Put the skills into practice

p.41-61

HOW TO USE THIS BOOK

4. EXPERIENCE
Take it to the next level
p.63-75

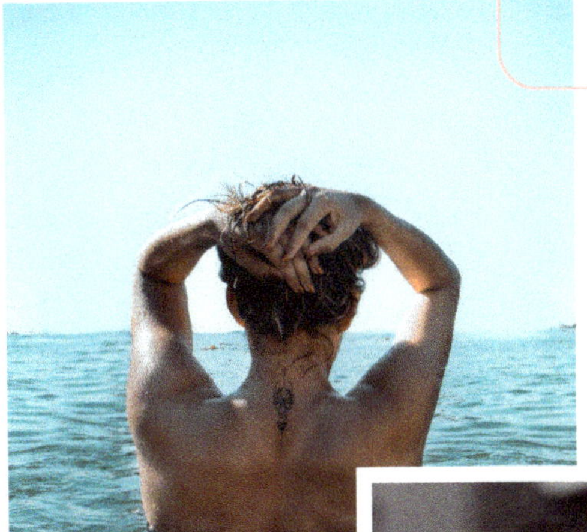

5. RESOURCES
Worksheets, posters and guides to refer back to on the journey
p.79-97

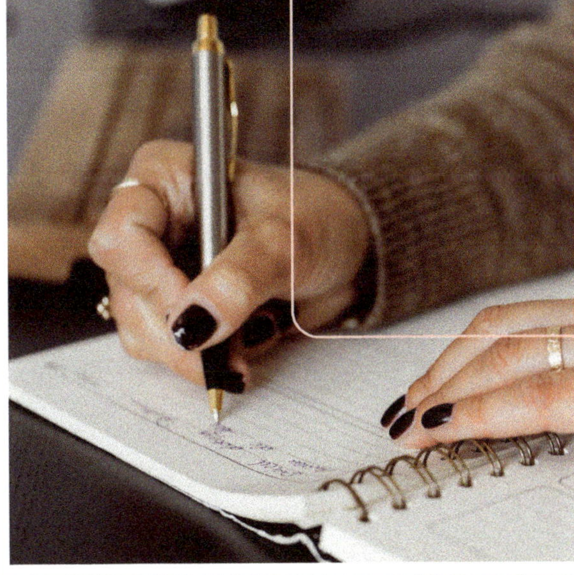

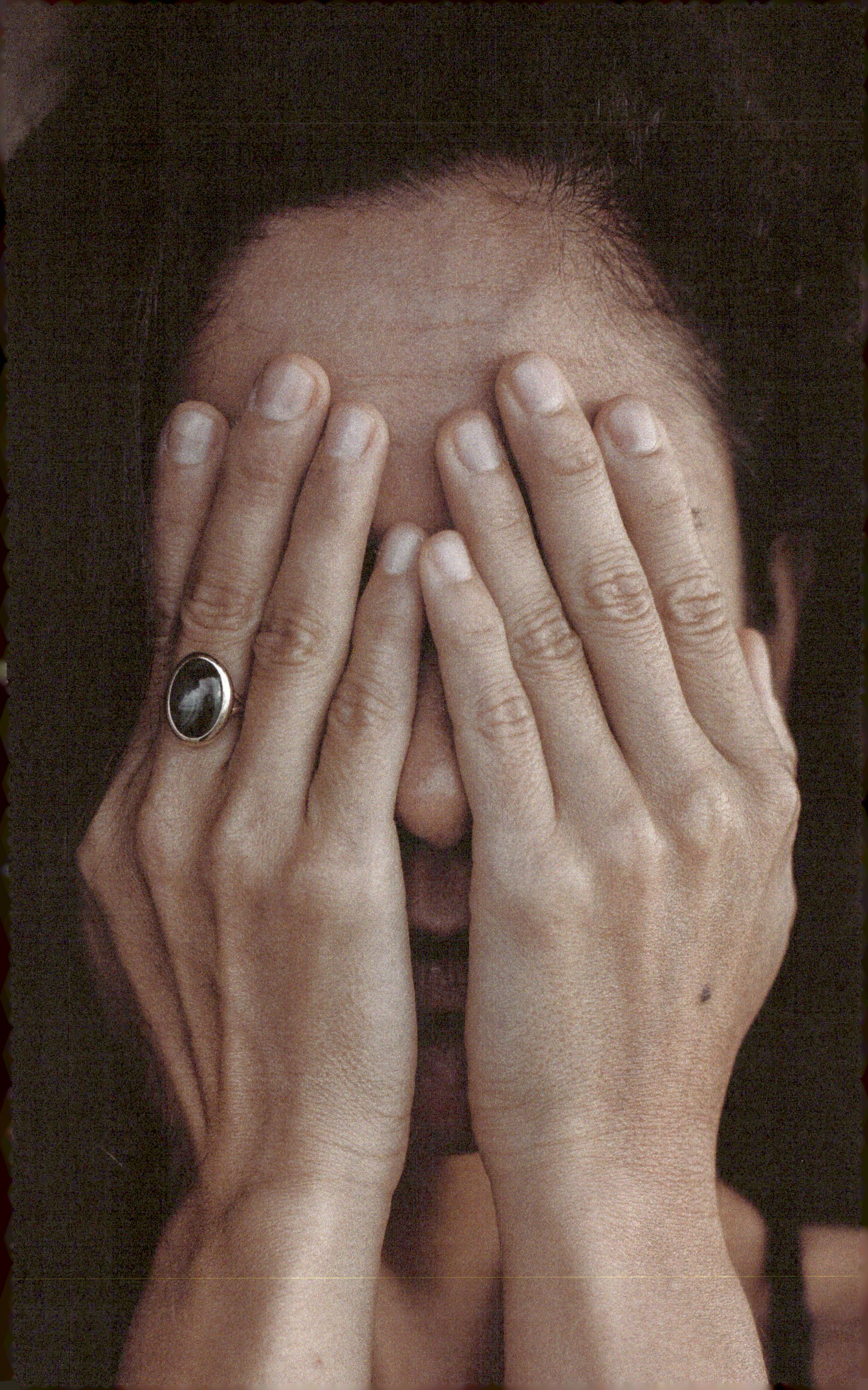

OH DEAR

I had just finished my graphic design degree, and I had my first 'real' paying customer. It was a simple job to design a business card, but for some reason whenever I opened my laptop to design it, I was bashed in the head with an intense resistance.

I couldn't ask myself where the resistance was coming from or why. It was such an uncomfortable feeling that I didn't even want to think about it, so I ran from it. I procrastinated, missed the deadline and dodged the client's phone calls. A week later they stopped calling, and I accepted defeat.

I had not only failed the client but my parents, who had supported me through a three-year university degree that I clearly didn't deserve. What kind of graphic designer can't even turn on their computer? After that early experience I decided I didn't have what it took to be a professional creative. I couldn't handle the pressure. I gave up.

There was relief in the failure, there was no longer any pressure to be perfect. With the pressure and resistance gone I was able to open the laptop and, to my surprise, finish the design quickly. I emailed it to the client with a long apology. They tried to pay me, but I was too embarrassed to take their money. What a mess.

It was my fear of failure that caused the resistance. A fear I had struggled with throughout my time at university. Sometimes it looked like procrastinating or playing small, and sometimes it turned me into a perfectionist control freak who over-delivered. Whatever I did to deal with the fear, it only got stronger.

My fear of failure made me quit graphic design after that first gig and pivot my career toward teaching. The old 'those who can't do, teach' scenario. The fear followed me into teaching, of course, but something interesting happened in the classroom.

I saw kids as young as twelve years old crippled by the same fear. And their fear seemed to get stronger each year they attended school. It was as if they came with bucket loads of imagination in year seven, and every year they lost a bit more. The year nines were especially anxious. After that most kids just stopped trying.

They wanted to know the 'right answer' before they would engage, even in the art classroom. I would tell them, 'There is no right or wrong answer' and that 'Mistakes are part of the process', but they looked back at me blankly.

It frustrated me that I couldn't get through to them, so I started doing research, which began my six-year obsession with the fear of failure. I discovered that the world had changed since I was a student. Two fundamental shifts were fueling my students' debilitating fear of failure.

High school has always been a self-conscious time where kids hustle to be liked and included by their peers, but now they had data. Teenagers had become hyper aware of their 'personal brands' as they counted their likes and followers on numerous social media platforms. Making a wrong move socially now had measurable implications. The pressure!

The focus of schooling had also subtly shifted away from learning and toward ranking. Standardised tests have always been a part of education. They're a great way for teachers to gauge how their students are performing based on the national average, but never before were the results published publicly for easy comparison.

Since 2010, the My Schools website has displayed and ranked the test results of every school in Australia. It had become a tool that parents used to decide which school they should send their children to. Schools also used the website's data to hire the highest-performing teachers. And governments used it to award high-achieving schools with more funding.

Scoring well on the test meant more enrollments (and more money) for schools and better jobs (and more money) for teachers. While schools and teachers felt pressure to raise their students' scores, the real pressure fell on the shoulders of the kids. The word 'NAPLAN'* was enough to invoke panic attacks in teenagers throughout Australia.

The My Schools website was inspired by America's 'No Child Left Behind Act'. It was implemented to create consistency across Australia's schooling and stop children from falling through the cracks of the education system. But this initiative, aiming to help children, was actually creating a new hurdle for them by sabotaging their mental health.

The focus on standardised testing conditioned students to believe there was only one right answer, when in life and creativity there is no such thing. There are multiple ways to skin a cat, a grotesque metaphor that was being lost on these kids who felt that one misstep was fatal.

I'm not talking about a little extra stress. These children were being traumatised every day they stepped into the classroom. The system that they lived and breathed taught them that their acceptance was conditional, with many students literally being encouraged to leave school early due to concerns they might bring down the school's average score.

Helicopter parenting gets a lot of blame for the sharp spike in student anxiety. While it's true that keeping kids away from struggle makes them more fragile, no amount of 'resilience' training can compete with this systemic trauma. No matter what I tried there were no quick fixes.

Thankfully, there are passionate researchers and education policy advocates, such as Dr Nicky Dulfer, who are fighting for the Australian education system to rethink its practices. But those changes will take time. Instead of waiting, let me share with you what I uncovered as I continued to research the fear of failure and how I eventually became 'Failure Friendly'.

**The National Assessment Program - Literacy and Numeracy (NAPLAN) is an annual national assessment for all students in Years 3, 5, 7, and 9. All students in these year levels are expected to participate in tests in reading, writing, language conventions (spelling, grammar and punctuation) and numeracy.*

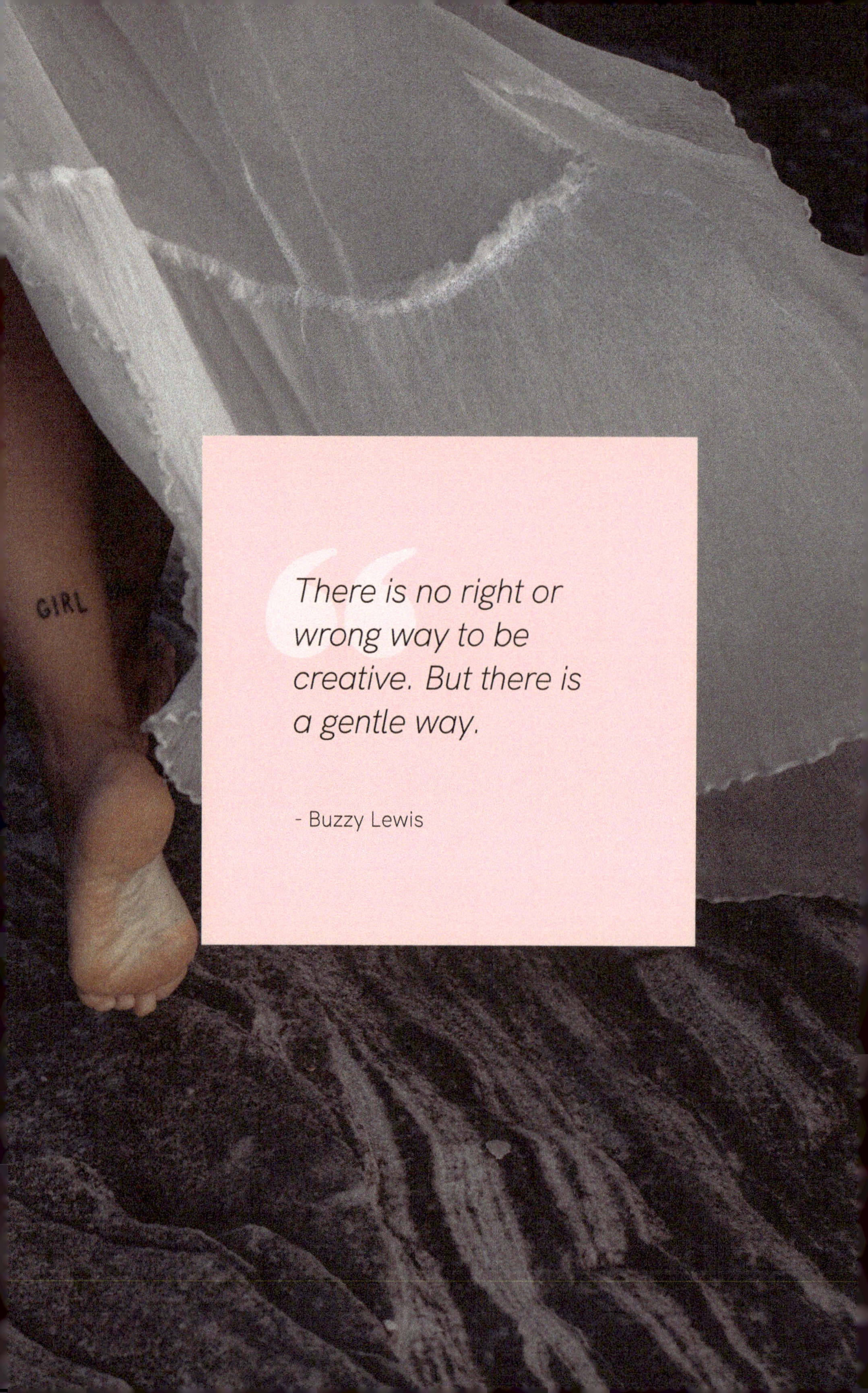
GIRL
There is no right or wrong way to be creative. But there is a gentle way.
- Buzzy Lewis

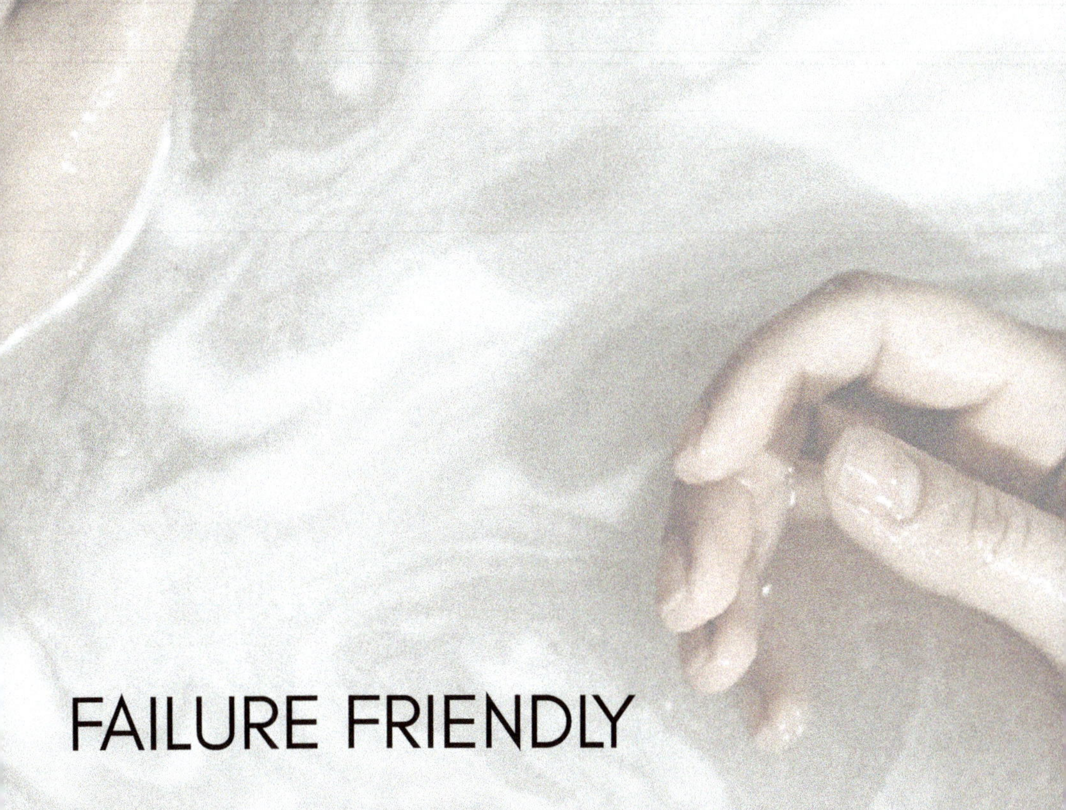

FAILURE FRIENDLY

Becoming Failure Friendly means mastering three important skills: self-awareness, self-belief and self-compassion. These skills are the remedy to our biggest blockers: self-consciousness, self-doubt and self-pity. When we clear these blocks, we uncover an unshakable trust in ourselves and the creative process, a compass to re-balance ourselves when the system makes us wobble.

By becoming Failure Friendly I have been able to reclaim my life. Not only have I enjoyed a thriving graphic design and marketing career, I have done things that I never thought were possible. I've sold my own artwork, I've started and run my own businesses and I've travelled the world. It's not what I've done but how I've done it that matters.

Whether you or someone you love wants to innovate, work in the arts, create content or solve real-world problems, it's important to know there is no right or wrong way to be creative. But there is a gentle way. A way that will nourish and sustain you along the path. If you or the creative person that you love is tired of fighting against our natural response to uncertainty, and you're ready for a friendlier way, read on!

MENTAL HEALTH CHECK

Second guessing yourself can look like:

- Indecision (I don't know)
- Apathy (I don't care)
- Rehearsing conversations in your mind
- Replaying conversation in your mind
- Imposter syndrome
- Over explaining and justifying yourself
- Speaking last or not at all in group settings
- Disclaimers, e.g., 'It's probably a stupid question'
- 'All or nothing' approaches (inability to accept uncertainty)
- Apologising, even for things that are out of your control
- An inability to deal with obstacles
- Asking others for their opinions instead of your own
- Oversharing and lack of boundaries
- Analysis paralysis, e. g., endless research and planning
- Checklists for your checklists
- Editing yourself and your ideas before exploring their potential
- Giving up on your ideas and yourself

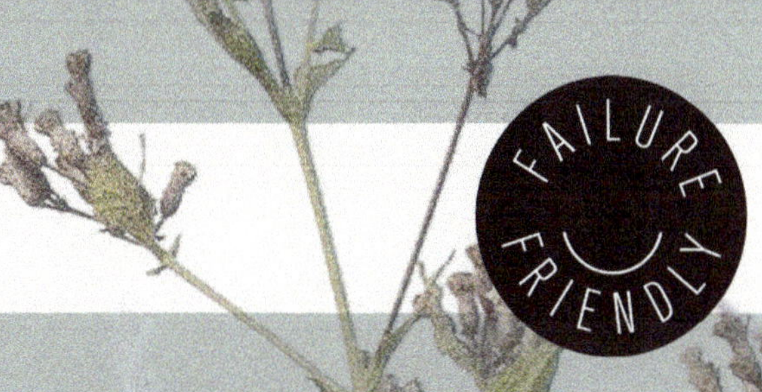

How often do you second guess yourself?

a) more than I used to
b) all the time
c) most of the time
d) some of the time
e) rarely

If your response was anything but e), this is a good indicator that you've been in a disempowering environment, and your mental health has room for improvement.

When we feel unsafe in ourselves and our surroundings, second-guessing is a way to protect ourselves and regain a sense of control. But second-guessing as a long-term solution leads to reduced confidence. No amount of money, education or talent can make up for poor confidence; it will always hold you back.

Healthy environments produce healthy people who trust themselves, so let's explore how to create healthy mindsets and supportive environments.

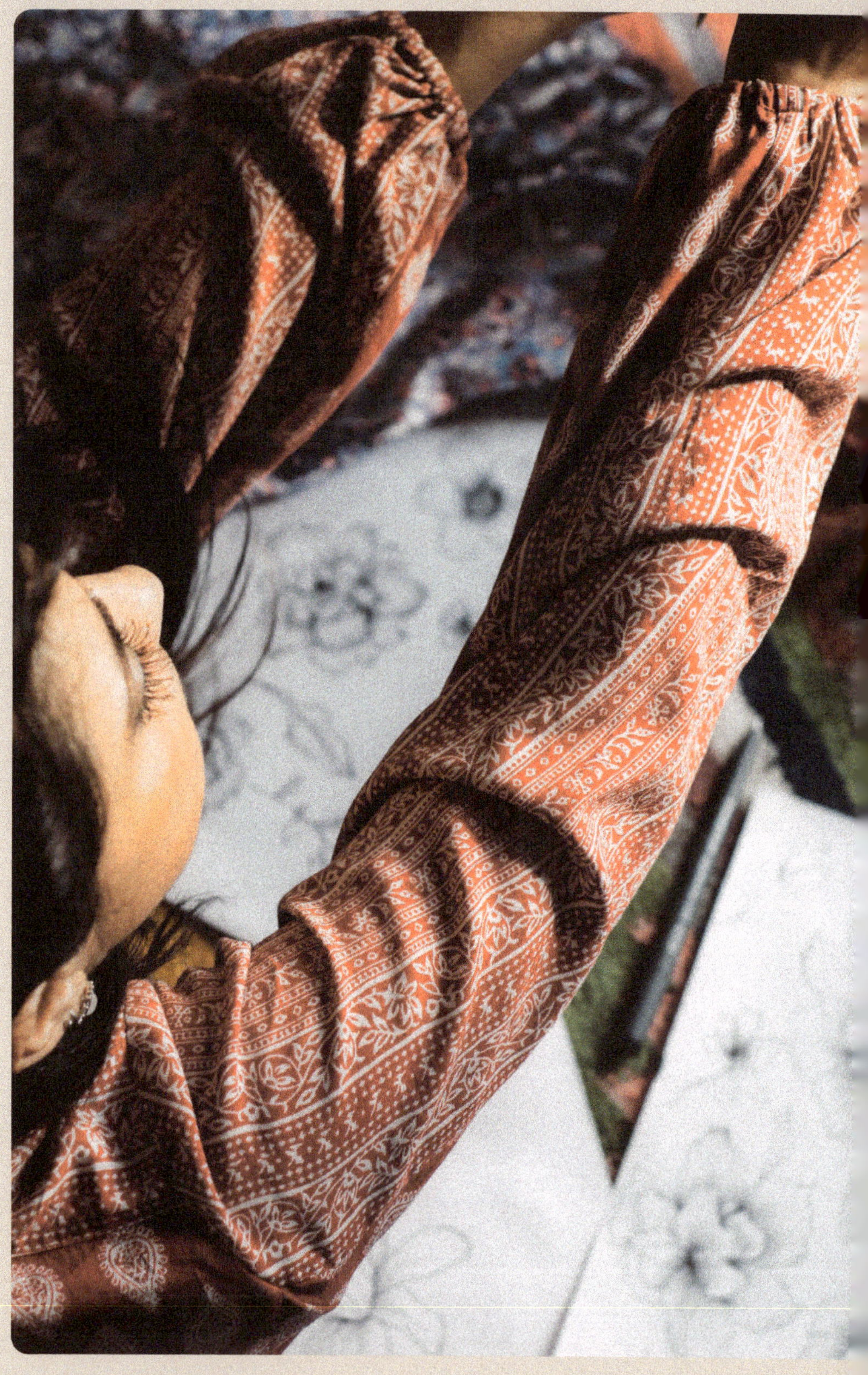

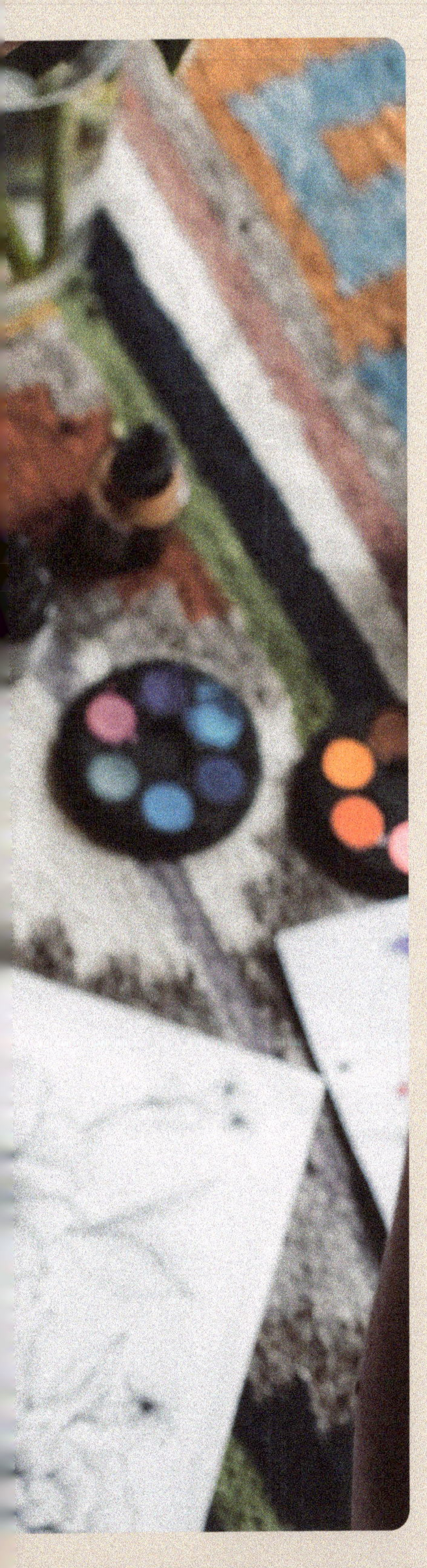

FRAMEWORK

The next section includes the initial insights and gold nuggets from my research into creative anxiety.

I've used these findings as a guide or a checklist for how to create a Failure Friendly space.

If you use this framework to set up your mind, work culture and physical space, you will create the structure needed to feel safe.

Only when we feel safe in ourselves and our environment are we able to relax, play, experiment, take risks, be vulnerable and be creative!

To set yourself up for a smoother ride, take your time here. Watch the video, and follow the journal prompts or discuss the points with your team to get clear on your own creative needs.

FAST FACTS

Artistic and creative skills are flexible, not fixed: Creativity is a muscle that grows with practice. Choosing a 'Growth Mindset' over a 'Fixed Mindset' is proven to increase happiness, resilience and performance.

Creativity is an essential skill for all students. More than half of today's students will work in jobs that have not yet been created. In a world of increasingly rapid change, students must be able to adapt to change, problem solve, be innovative and in many cases create their own jobs.

Creativity is something you do, it's not who you are. You don't stop being when you stop creating. Attaching your identity to your creativity is a slippery slope to conditional self-acceptance, self-judgment and a whole lot of suffering. Letting creativity be your practice, not your identity, helps to grow resilience.

Creative people, that is people who do creative work and who work in arts-related jobs, are statically more likely to commit suicide as a result of mental illness. Many creative people are afflicted with the 'Artist's Ego', a desire for individualisation or wanting to be different from the crowd, which leads many creatives to feel isolated and alone. Creatives are more sensitive than the average person. This is part of their gift to notice inspiration and connections that others miss. They experience major shifts in mood and energy that change like the tides. It's common for them to experience a 'flow state' where they can work without rest or food for long periods, followed by long periods of rest. The rest periods are just as important as the creative work. Nine-to-five productivity-obsessed work cultures do not suit most creative people's nature.

Rules and structure make us feel safe. Studies show that when children have clear boundaries, they feel safe and are more likely to be playful and adventurous—important ingredients for creativity! Exposure therapy has long been a successful tool for overcoming fear. When children are exposed to the creative process with structured and incremental activities, they naturally grow their confidence and willingness to engage in the process. (Emotional safety is everything!).

The creative process requires us to step into uncertainty and make mistakes, which naturally causes anxiety. The creative process, or the process of change, follows a predictable curve that begins with high emotions in the ideas stage. Things get increasingly more difficult as we step further into the process until we hit a low emotional state that triggers a point of acceptance. This is the halfway point. Once we accept that we are not fully in control, we begin to embrace the uncertainty with play and discovery, which leads to learning and achieving success which produces positive emotions that peak at the finish line. Each time we move through the process, we grow our skills and confidence, but it is impossible to completely bypass the 'dark side' of creativity. Watch a video about this at **failurefriendly.com/process.**

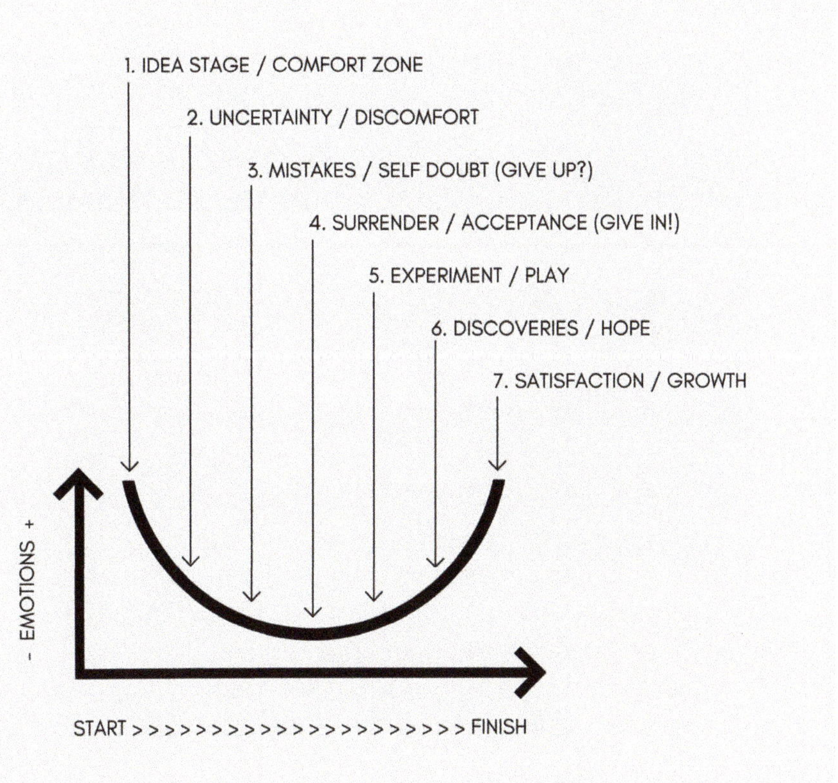

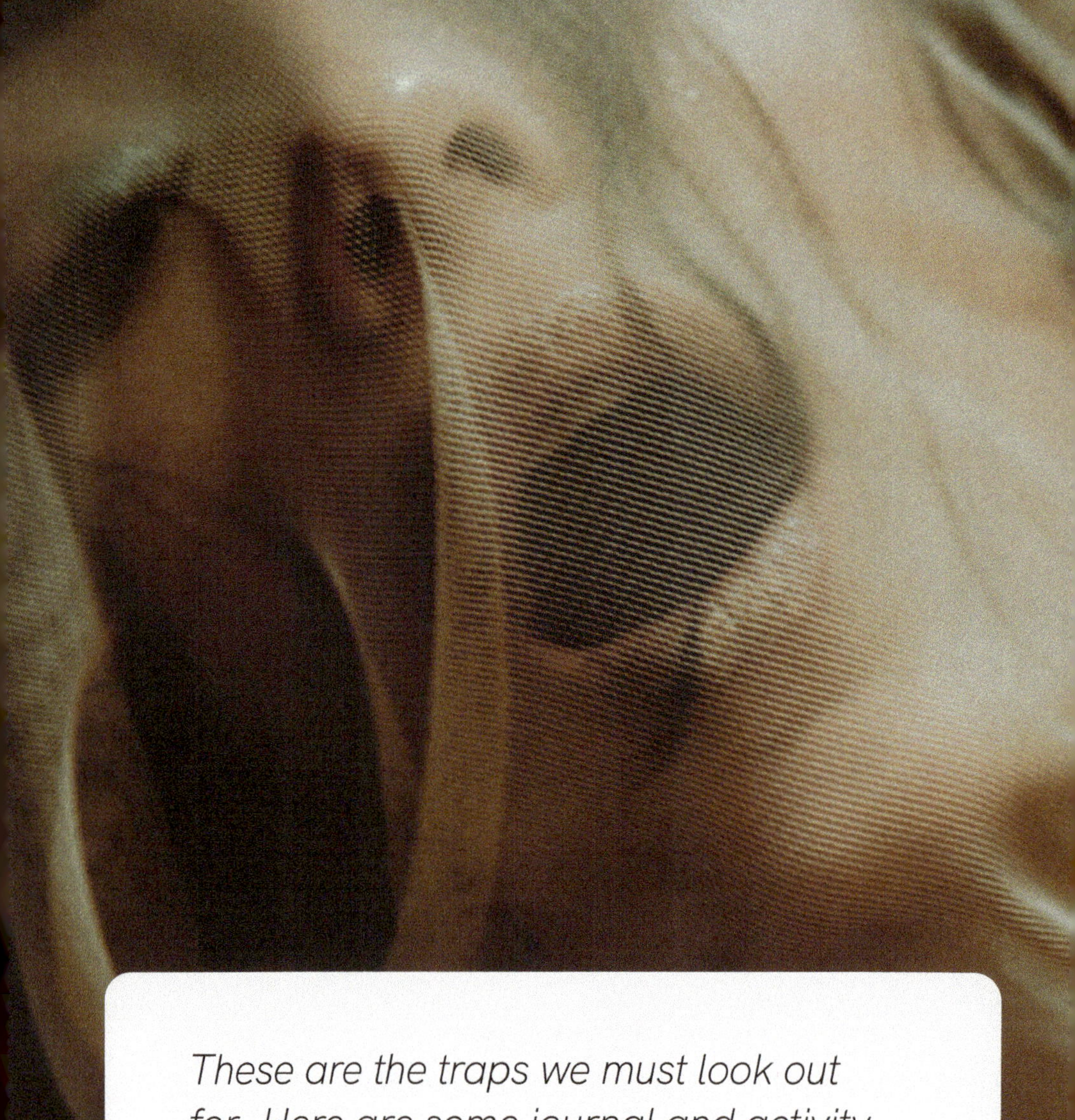

These are the traps we must look out for. Here are some journal and activity prompts to prepare yourself.

- Can you think of an example or behaviour for each trap?
- Why are these behaviours so tempting?
- Why are these traps problematic?
- What would the opposite behaviour be for each trap?
- Which traps do you commonly fall into?
- What do you need in order to avoid these temptations?
- How can you help those who've fallen into these traps?

TRAPS

Talent is something we have no control over. When we pin our success on our God-given talent or our failure on our lack of it, we have little motivation to persevere and grow. But grow we can when we focus on things we can control, such as technique, effort and persistence.

Perfectionism is the fear of never being good enough. People with this affliction hide their fear by avoiding challenges that could expose them or by over-worrying, over-working and over-delivering to compensate for their perceived inadequacies, which leads to burnout because whatever they do achieve is never good enough in their eyes. Turning our attention to healing the wounded part of us that feels not good enough using self-compassion will free us up to focus on progress rather than perfection.

Critical self-talk robs us of momentum and the feel-good hormone dopamine that we get when we achieve a goal. Instead of discounting our efforts with self-criticism, we must count all achievements, no matter how big or small. It's proven that when we celebrate our wins with gratitude practices, we are more likely to achieve our next goal. This is because our brain craves another dopamine reward, meaning it will subconsciously look for possibilities instead of reasons to give up.

Intellectualising or sending the mind to do the body's work is a recipe for disaster. Self-doubt and self-pity are vicious thought cycles that happen in the mind. They go around and around with no end in sight. That's why they keep us stuck. Instead of thinking about the discomfort we feel in ourselves (self-doubt) or dwelling on the pain we feel in the process (self-pity), we can invite these feelings into our bodies where they are processed and released. As they say, 'You gotta feel it to heal it'.

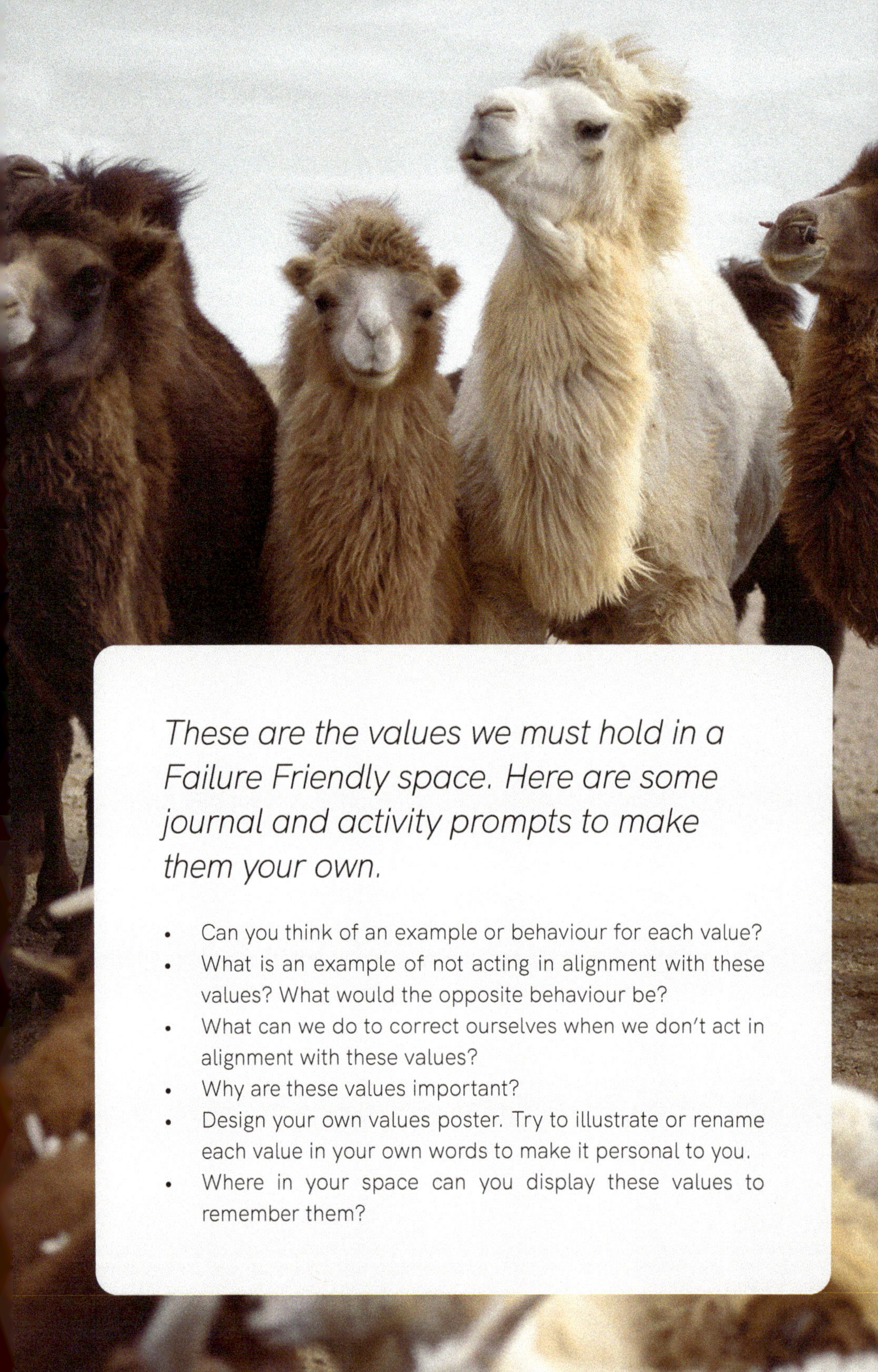

These are the values we must hold in a Failure Friendly space. Here are some journal and activity prompts to make them your own.

- Can you think of an example or behaviour for each value?
- What is an example of not acting in alignment with these values? What would the opposite behaviour be?
- What can we do to correct ourselves when we don't act in alignment with these values?
- Why are these values important?
- Design your own values poster. Try to illustrate or rename each value in your own words to make it personal to you.
- Where in your space can you display these values to remember them?

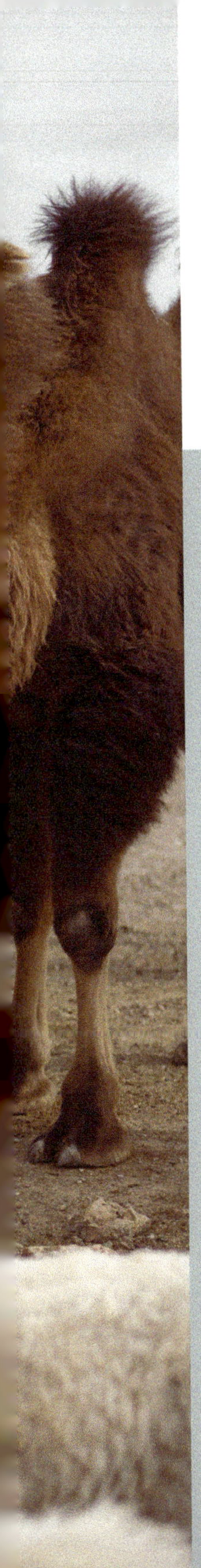

VALUES

Risk Taking

When the goal is to create something new, risk taking is essential.

Friendliness

Risk taking requires a high level of emotional support, both internally and externally.

Openness

Perfectionism is the enemy of creativity. Learn to delay judgement by aiming for drafts, experiments and trials. Give yourself permission to be clumsy.

Curiosity

Mistakes are a necessary part of the learning and creative process. Rename mistakes as 'discoveries', and celebrate them as you learn.

Play

Play is the biggest driver for innovation. It can unlock creative confidence and disable rigid perfectionism.

Engagement

Paying attention, being completely engaged in the creative process or in a 'flow state', is more rewarding than getting attention. For authenticity seek the pleasure of the process over the praise of the product.

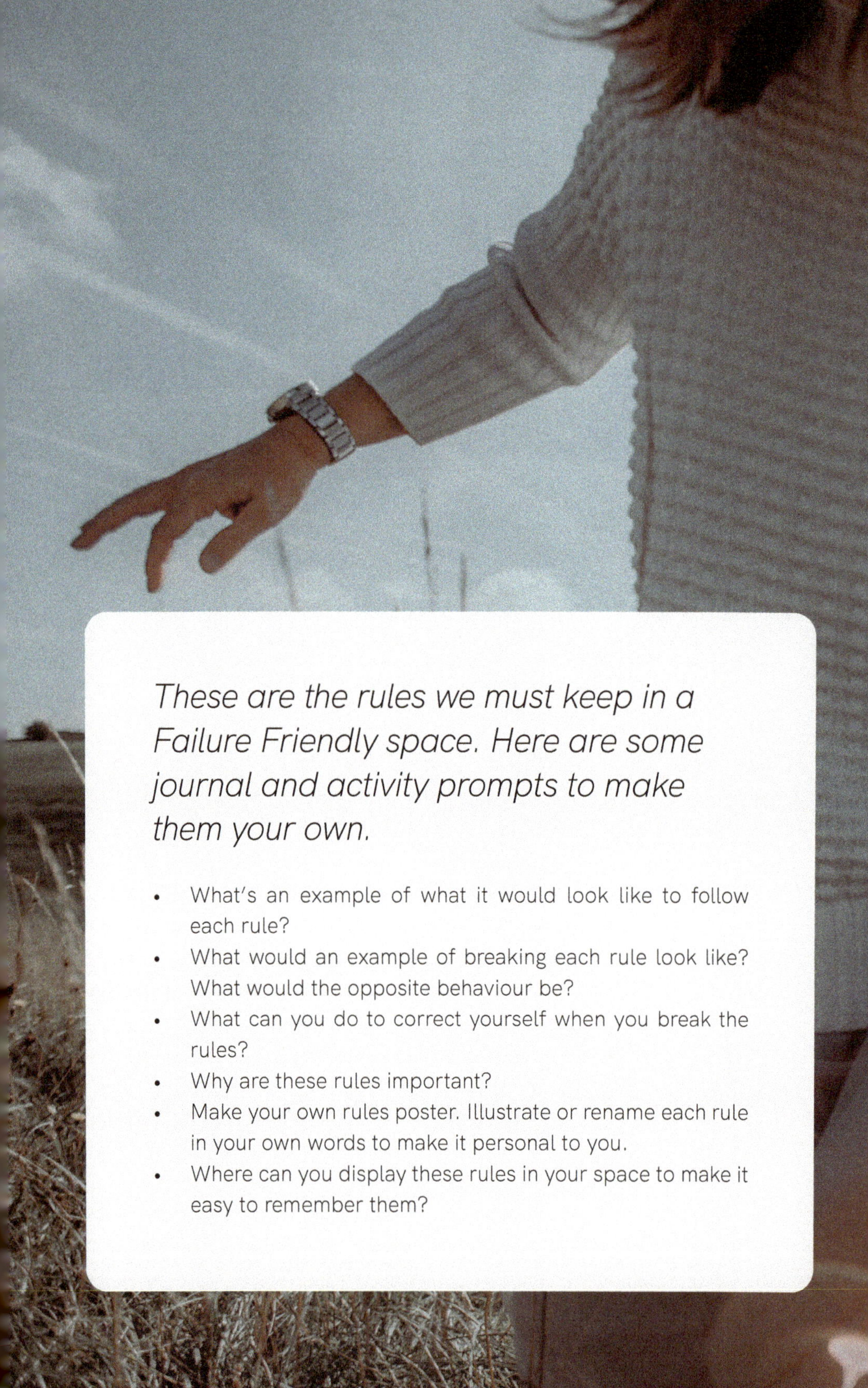

These are the rules we must keep in a Failure Friendly space. Here are some journal and activity prompts to make them your own.

- What's an example of what it would look like to follow each rule?
- What would an example of breaking each rule look like? What would the opposite behaviour be?
- What can you do to correct yourself when you break the rules?
- Why are these rules important?
- Make your own rules poster. Illustrate or rename each rule in your own words to make it personal to you.
- Where can you display these rules in your space to make it easy to remember them?

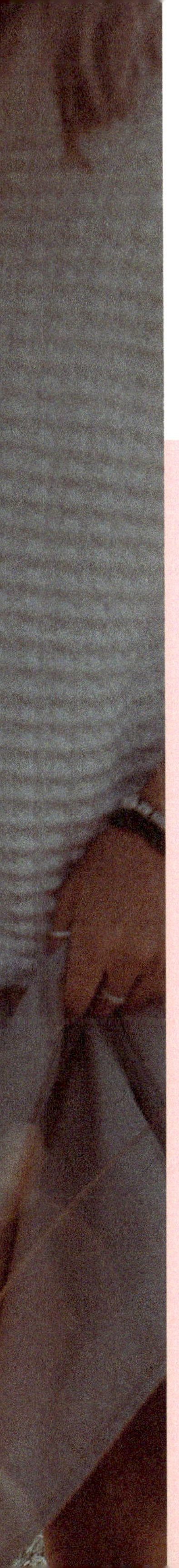

RULES

Everybody is accepted

Creative spaces don't judge, blame or shame. Ideas can be shared by anyone at any time, but we only share advice when we are asked for our opinion.

Positive language only

To stay resilient in the face of creative anxiety we must maintain positive and helpful self-talk. If you wouldn't say it to a friend, don't say it to yourself. By putting the word 'yet' at the end of a sentence like 'I don't know how to yet' we open up a world of positive possibilities.

Separate the behaviour from the identity

Just because we have failed does not mean we are a 'failure'. Watch the meaning you make of things by remembering that situations are temporary experiences that do not define us.

Go for quantity

Every good idea is the result of at least ten bad ones. This is called the 'ideas funnel'. First attempts and bad ideas are reasons to celebrate, the more the merrier!

Encourage wild ideas

Wild ideas give rise to creative leaps in thinking. When faced with a dismissive thought like 'I can't' or 'It's not possible', instead ask yourself 'How can I?' or 'What if?'

Constructive praise only

Constructive praise focuses on what can be controlled. Critiques should speak to growth, not talent. Rather than 'You're so gifted', praise technique or specific behaviours like effort and persistence. (Or, ideally, avoid praise altogether and focus on the pleasure of the process! Instead of 'Good job!' try 'You did it! How do you feel?', 'How did you do that?' or 'What did you learn?')

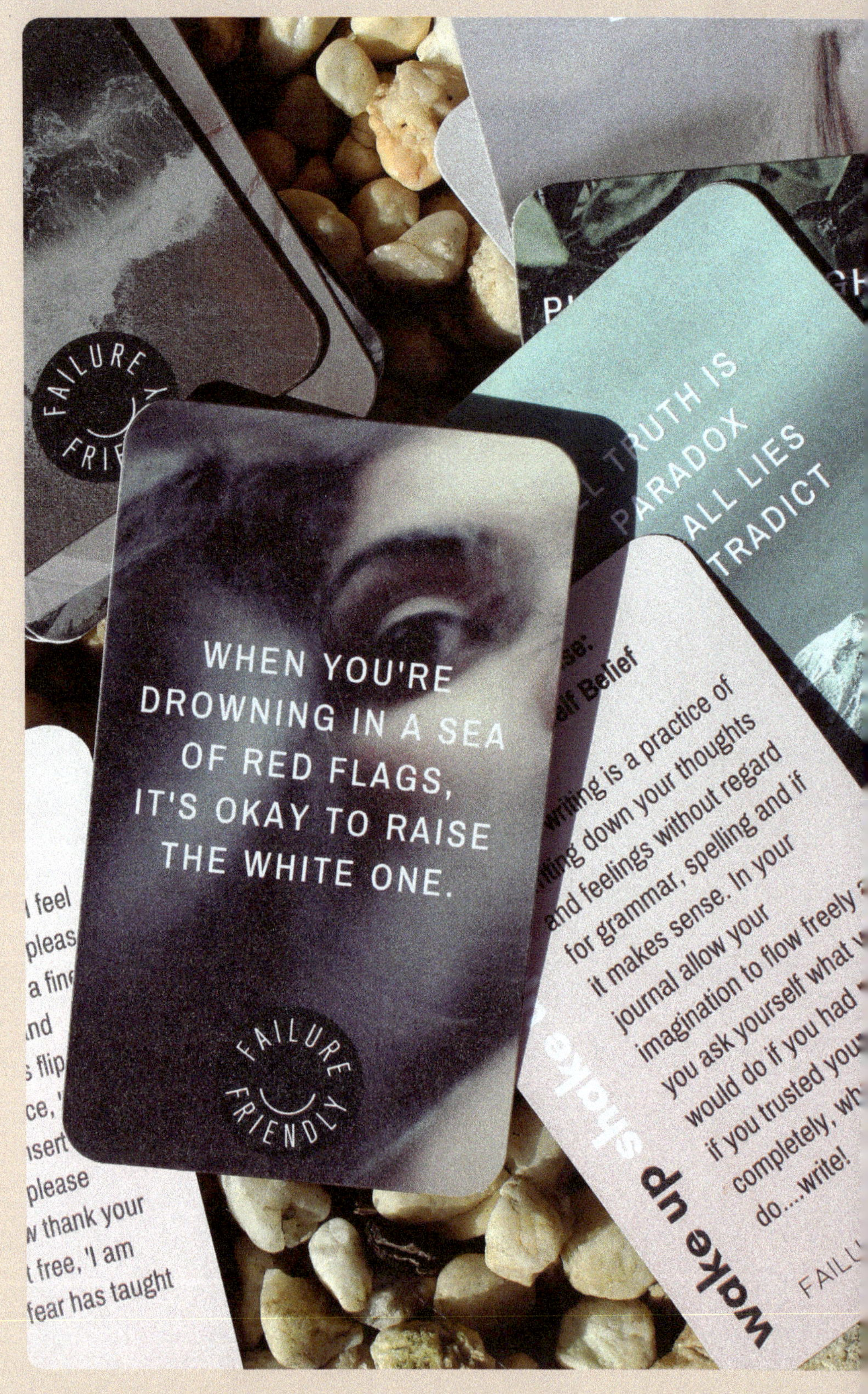
WHEN YOU'RE DROWNING IN A SEA OF RED FLAGS, IT'S OKAY TO RAISE THE WHITE ONE.
FAILURE FRIENDLY
wake up

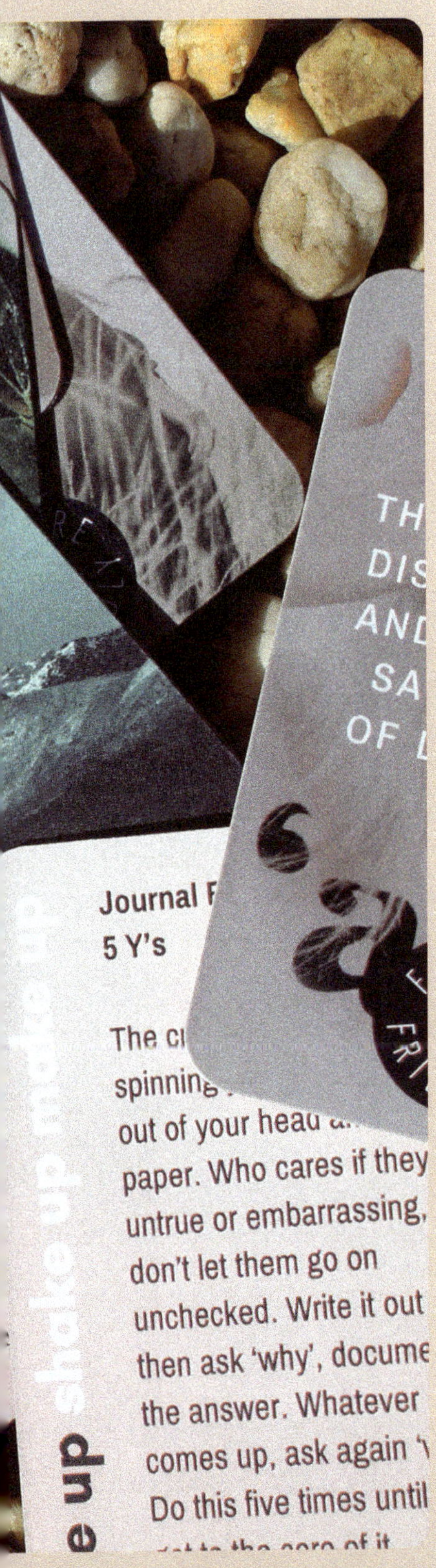

SKILL SET

In the next section, I have tried to peel back the layers of the three greatest blockers to creative confidence and how we can treat the causes rather than just the symptoms.

Self-awareness, self-belief and self-compassion may sound like vague and lofty skills to grasp, let alone master. We can read about them all we like, but it's not until we start acting them out and experiencing them that we truly understand what they are.

This is why I created the Failure Friendly Action Cards. In this deck of twenty-one cards you will find seven activities for practicing self-awareness, seven hands-on exercises for self-belief and seven practical ways to embody self-compassion. Each activity builds upon the one before to cement the learning.

In this section I have included links to twenty-one audio recordings that accompany each action card in the deck. These recordings will guide you through each activity with in-depth explanations and examples. *Enjoy!*

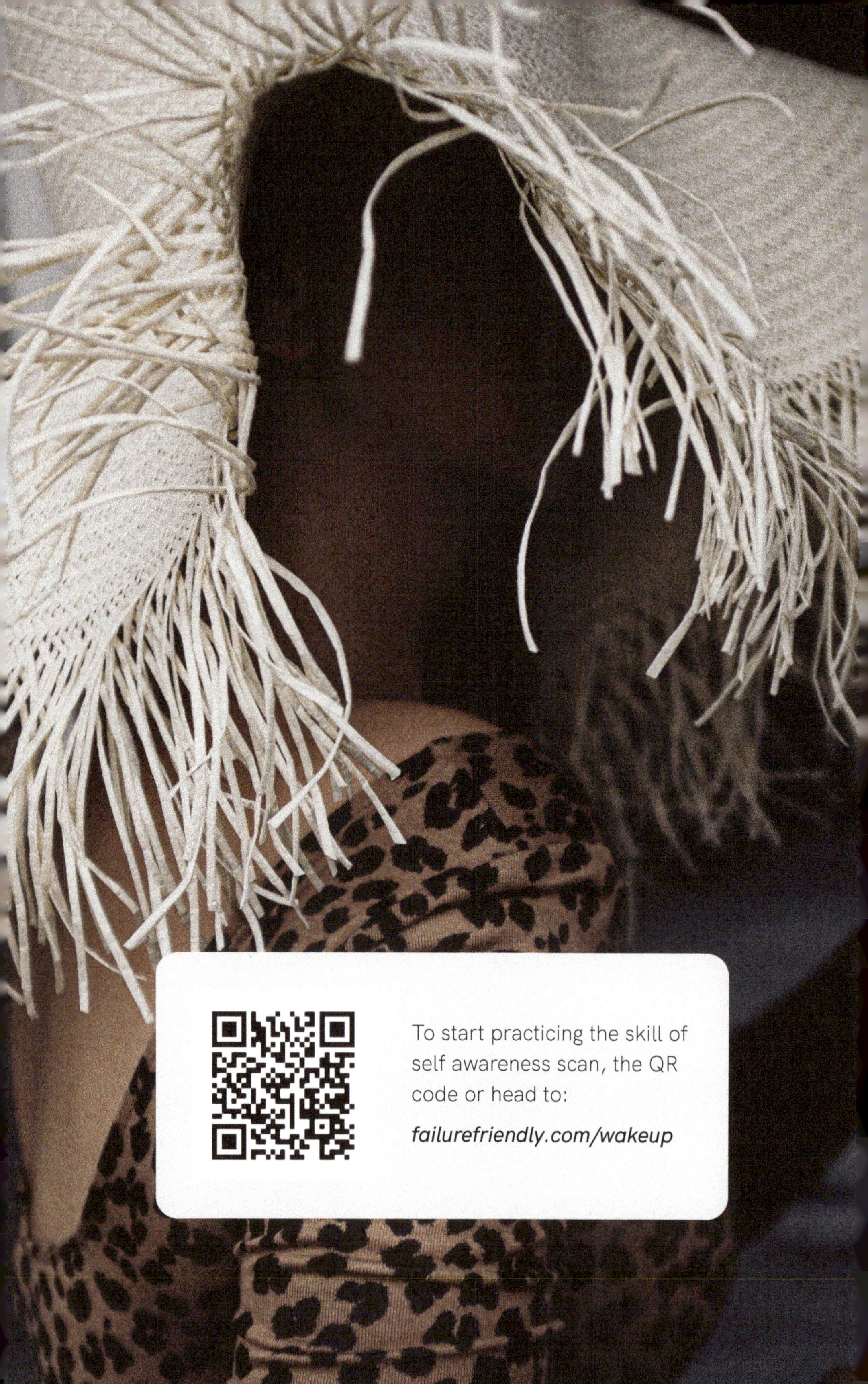
To start practicing the skill of self awareness scan, the QR code or head to:
failurefriendly.com/wakeup

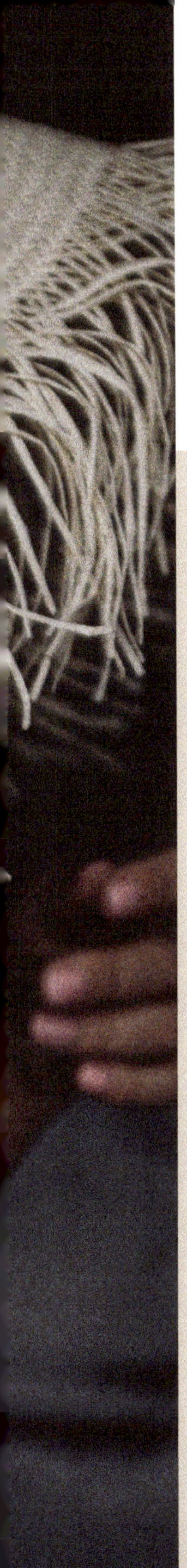

WAKE UP

Self-consciousness comes from insecurity. It signals that as a child we experienced distress when our needs were not met. We may not have been seen, heard, validated, understood or accepted. We may have even been ignored, shamed, rejected or abused for being ourselves.

Unable to see outside of ourselves, as children, we interpret the failure to have our needs met as something we have done wrong. Or that there's something wrong with us. To protect ourselves from repeating this painful experience we developed a hyper awareness of ourselves. In an effort to predict and control future rejections, we begin reading the room, comparing ourselves and analysing the meaning of our thoughts and behaviours.

Self-awareness is a distinctly different skill that involves witnessing our thoughts and behaviours without judgment. When we are self-aware, we can have negative or egoic thoughts without getting attached to what they mean and let them go just as quickly as they appear. Rather than reading the room we can centre ourselves and look inward for the answers.

The Wake Up card activities are designed to help you to tune into your self-talk and mental patterns, to identify which beliefs are holding you back.

Self-awareness is the most important skill of all. It is the starting point to uncover our limiting beliefs, without which we wouldn't be able to transform them into more empowering thoughts and behaviours. Self-awareness is also the tool we use to stay in alignment. It helps us to see when we begin to wobble and how we need to make changes to rebalance ourselves.

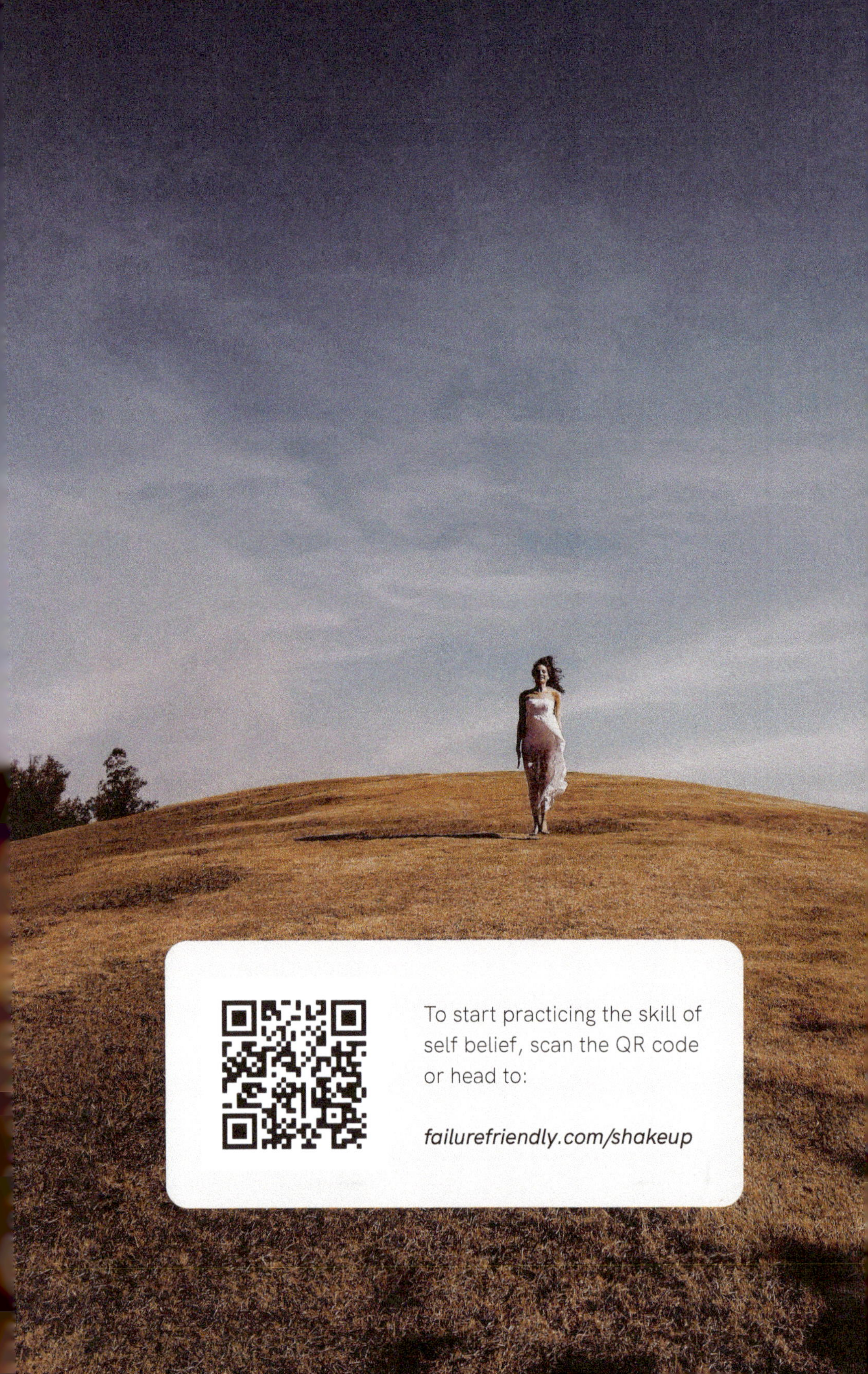
To start practicing the skill of
self belief, scan the QR code
or head to:
failurefriendly.com/shakeup

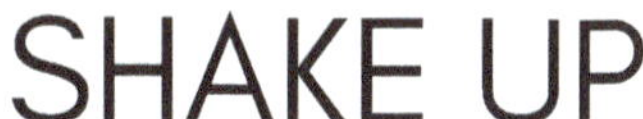

SHAKE UP

Self-doubt comes from a lack of trust in ourselves. It is a signal that the masculine part of us is disempowered.

Whatever our gender, we've all felt the thrill of our own masculine energy. Maybe you feel it when you workout, rev an engine or sign up for a challenge. It's the part of us that gets a kick out of taking action and risks.

To take risks we need a strong trust in ourselves, our abilities and resilience. Without this self-belief we don't feel safe internally, so we develop coping mechanisms to control ourselves rather than trust ourselves.

This can look like perfectionism or over-delivering because we believe our best may not be good enough, playing small and only signing up for challenges that do not stretch us. It can also look like procrastinating or removing ourselves from uncertainty by giving up on the challenge.

These behaviours become habits that strengthen the limiting belief that we are not to be trusted. Rather than using Band-Aid solutions like positive affirmations, the Shake Up action card exercises explore how our need for approval is at the core of our self-doubt.

With self-belief we can start to take confident action from a place of self-approval. No longer will the opinions of others affect whether or not we have a go. And setting and holding boundaries will become effortless.

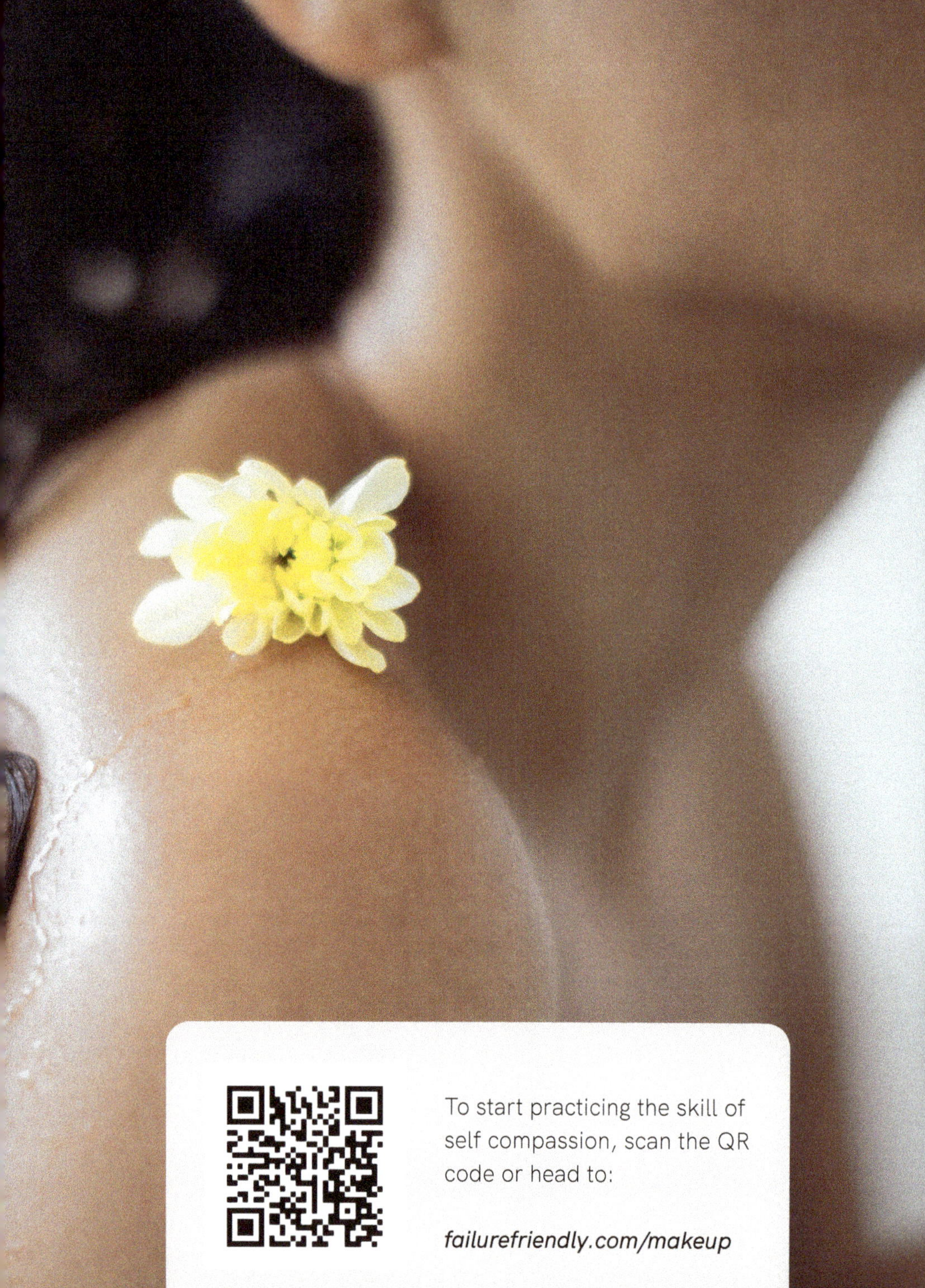

To start practicing the skill of self compassion, scan the QR code or head to:

failurefriendly.com/makeup

MAKE UP

Self-pity comes from a lack of trust in the process. It signals that the feminine part of us is disempowered.

Whatever our gender, we've all felt the flow of our own feminine energy. Maybe you feel it when you float in a body of water, when you nurture a plant or animal or when you lose yourself in creativity. It's the part of us that enjoys letting go.

In order to let go, surrender and receive we need to trust what we're receiving. This is the part of us that can hold space for uncertainty and take what comes, whether that's inspiration or disaster. It's a soothing energy that says, 'It's okay', when we feel pain and reassures us that even in failure, we are enough.

Without self-compassion we don't feel safe in the process, or externally, so we develop coping mechanisms to control the process rather than trust it. This can look like putting up walls, going inside ourselves and hiding, or blaming and shaming the mistakes of others to distance ourselves from the problem.

These behaviours become habits that strengthen the limiting belief that the world is out to get us, and the process cannot be trusted. Rather than using empty self-care practices like bubble baths and massages, the Make Up action card exercises explore how our need to work so hard to feel loveable is at the core of our self-pity.

When we give ourselves permission to honour who we really are rather than being what we think others need us to be, we reconnect with our internal compass and our humanity. Seeing yourself as an equal to others will make meeting your own needs come naturally. You will be open to receiving and putting yourself out there.

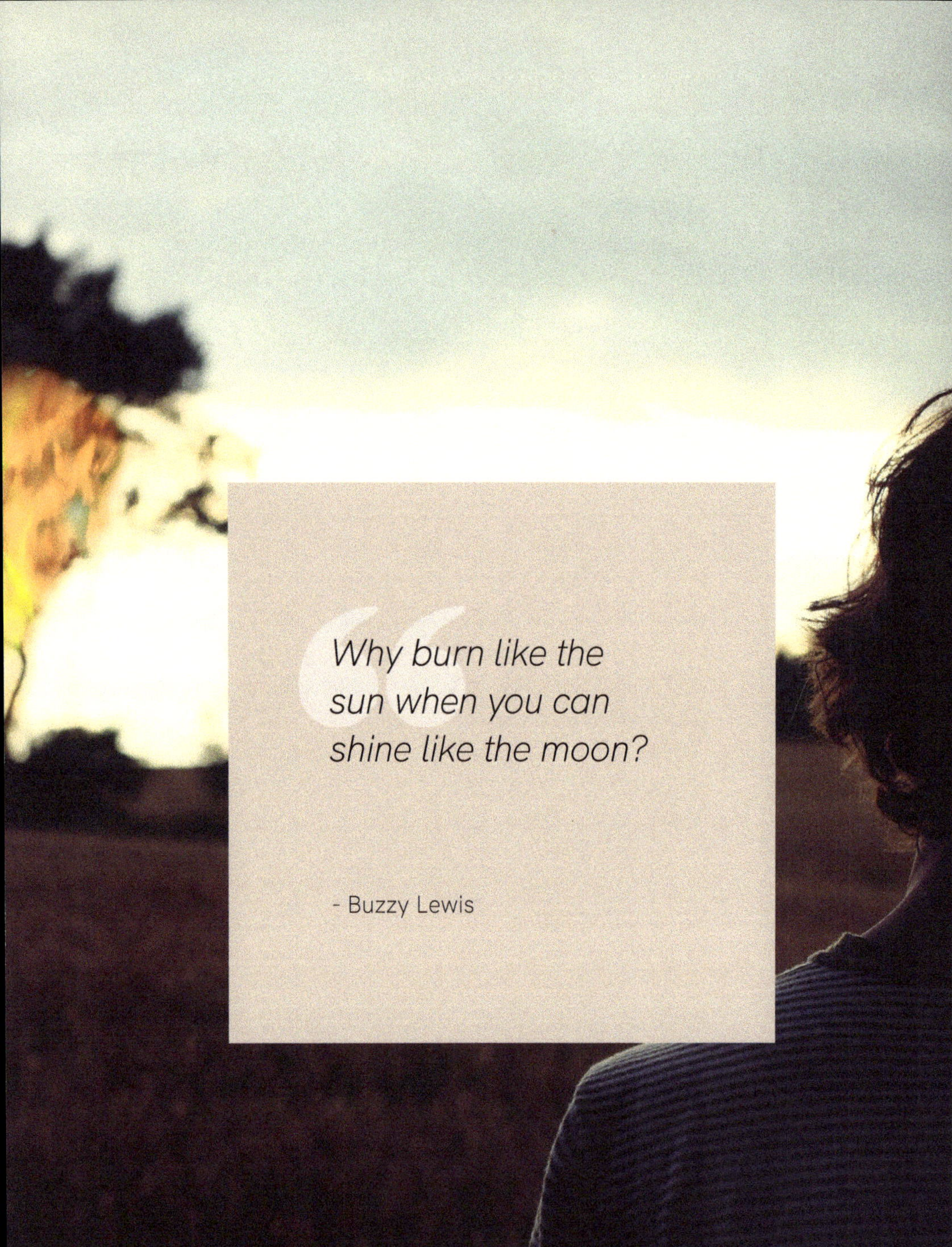
Why burn like the
sun when you can
shine like the moon?
- Buzzy Lewis

BURNOUT

Before I started practicing these skills, I had written so many cover letters that I never sent due to fear that I wasn't good enough. I turned down invitations to go travelling with friends because I couldn't fathom saving that much money, and the thought of being out in the big, scary world without parental supervision felt like a disaster waiting to happen. I wrote entire books and never showed them to a soul. And I had stopped sharing my art on social media because I didn't want my friends to think of me as a desperate attention seeker. I was the definition of playing small.

Within two years of using the tools outlined in this book, I had completed a master's research thesis and networked myself into a marketing manager job I was not even remotely qualified for. After a year of 'faking it till I made it' in that job, it no longer scared me. So, I did the next scariest thing on my list and went backpacking around India and Europe for six months. Two weeks after I returned to Australia, I had a stall at a local market selling my original art prints, and I surpassed my goal of breaking even. Not long after that I launched my own branding agency and purchased a second ecommerce business. I had become a ballsy entrepreneur juggling two businesses and speaking publicly at networking events. I was a girl on fire.

(Trigger warning: suicidal thoughts & domestic violence)

I had a 'Mindset Monday' ritual that I kept religiously. It started with the 'Face, Flip & Free' activity you'll find in the resources section of this book. By checking in with my fear at the start of the week, I was able to flip it into excitement and then use that excitement to break through my comfort zone to the next challenge. I primed my mind for action with dopamine-stacking practices like the 'Progress Party' worksheet. By focusing my mind on progress and momentum, I continued to accelerate my growth.

Free moments away from my computer or client meetings were spent listening to entrepreneurial podcasts. Richard Branson, Gary Vaynerchuk and Tony Robbins were my idols. They taught me to push harder, never give up and rest when you're dead. Being in this masculine energy was intoxicating. It made me feel in control and bad-ass. I even began to apply these positive psychology techniques to my health. Whenever I got a headache from looking at the screen, back pain from sitting at my desk, or just felt run down by my enormous workload, I would visualise healing and focus my mind on something positive.

Those two years of accelerated personal growth ended with me being bedridden for over a month. I had so much passion and endless ideas for the businesses, but after a year of burning the candle at both ends, I didn't have one shred of energy to make those ideas happen. The businesses had become my life, and being unable to work on them led me to dark suicidal thoughts.

I had used the Shake Up practices to bypass all of my negative emotions and bio-hack my dopamine levels, to the point that I now had adrenal fatigue. My body had been telling me for months to slow down, but I had made an art of suppressing its messages. The scary part was that I'd also used these tools to ignore the red flags in my personal life.

As I built up my businesses and reputation, my boyfriend at the time began to feel emasculated. In a subconscious and toxic attempt to restore the balance, he began to gaslight me. The abuse was insidious, and by the time I realised how bad it was, I believed that I deserved it, and, worse, I chose to see it as another growth opportunity to be grateful for.

Positive psychology hacks can liberate you, but they can also imprison you if you're not careful. My burnout taught me that I had 'femininity' all wrong. My 'don't run like a girl' upbringing and the overly masculine entrepreneurial content I was consuming taught me that action was the only thing that mattered. It also taught me that rest was for the weak, and crying or expressing negative emotions was the ultimate sign of weakness.

I clung to the sense of control these tools were giving me because I thought letting go would prove that I was weak. I thought admitting weakness was admitting that I didn't deserve my success. I thought it would expose me for the imposter I really was. I thought it meant losing everything I had built.

But the opposite was actually true.

When burnout forced me to surrender to my dark emotions, I discovered that rest and reflection were the vehicle to healing and greater strength, not weakness. I also learned that letting go feels so damn good. In the compassionate feminine space of surrender, pain isn't scary. Nothing can really hurt you there because pain is rich with wisdom and connection and soothing release. It's the very medicine we need to regain our equilibrium.

This is why the Make Up activities for self-compassion are so important. Dopamine is a powerful fire starter for when we feel stuck, but the goal is not to continue adding fuel to the fire until we reach a point of burnout. The self-compassion activities are designed to release a different neurotransmitter called oxytocin, or the 'love hormone'. Oxytocin is released when we hug someone. We can give it to ourselves when we place a hand on our heart, validate our emotions or 'soften and soothe'.

Oxytocin lowers stress and anxiety. It helps us rest or sleep better, and it has the power to regulate our emotional responses and pro-social behaviours, such as trust and empathy. It's a powerful anti-burnout medicine that reminds us we are more than just a content factory and that it's okay to feel difficult emotions and the need for rest. These feminine practices help us trust our true nature and honour the fullness of our human experience, both the 'positive' and the 'negative' - the action and the reflection.

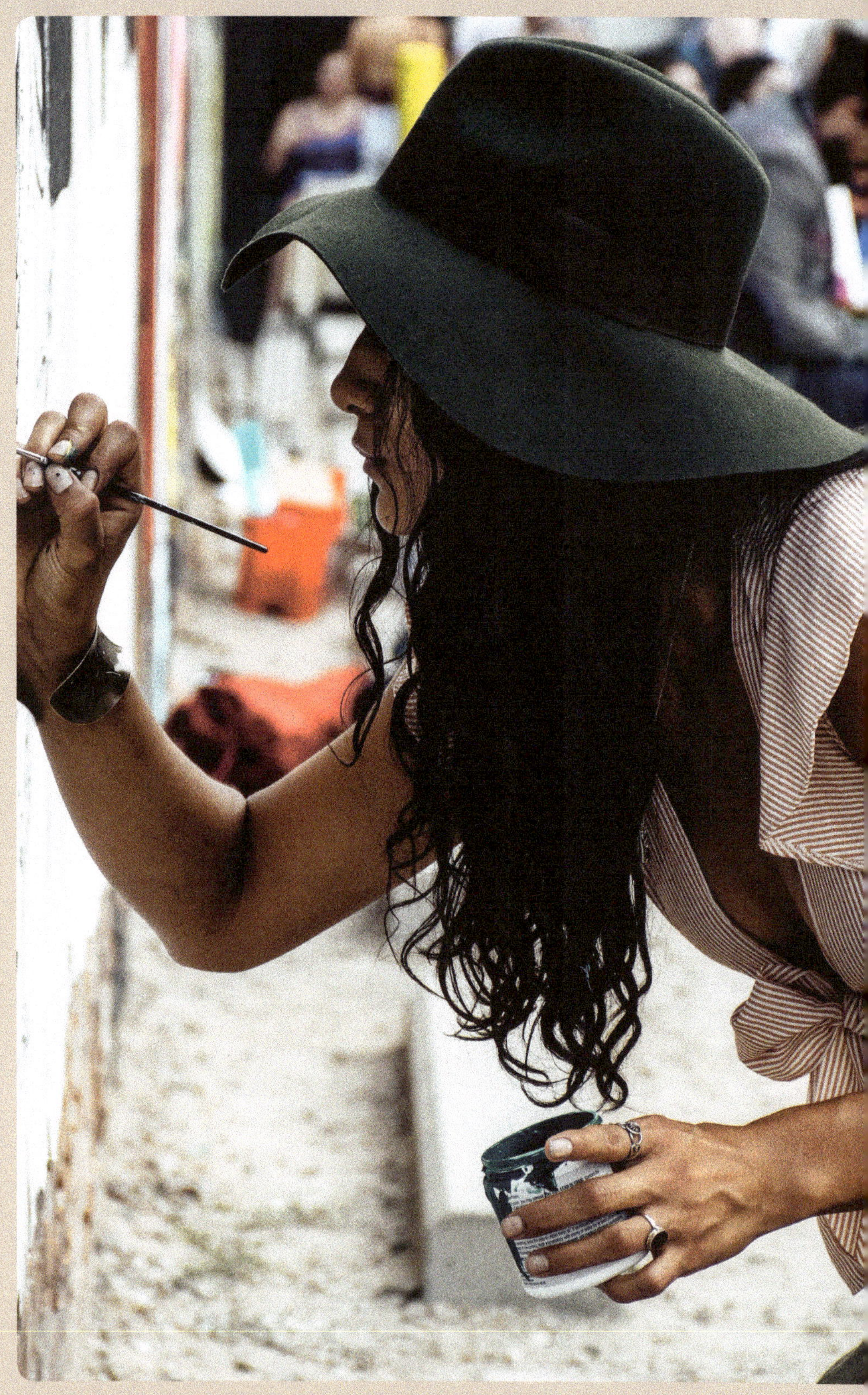

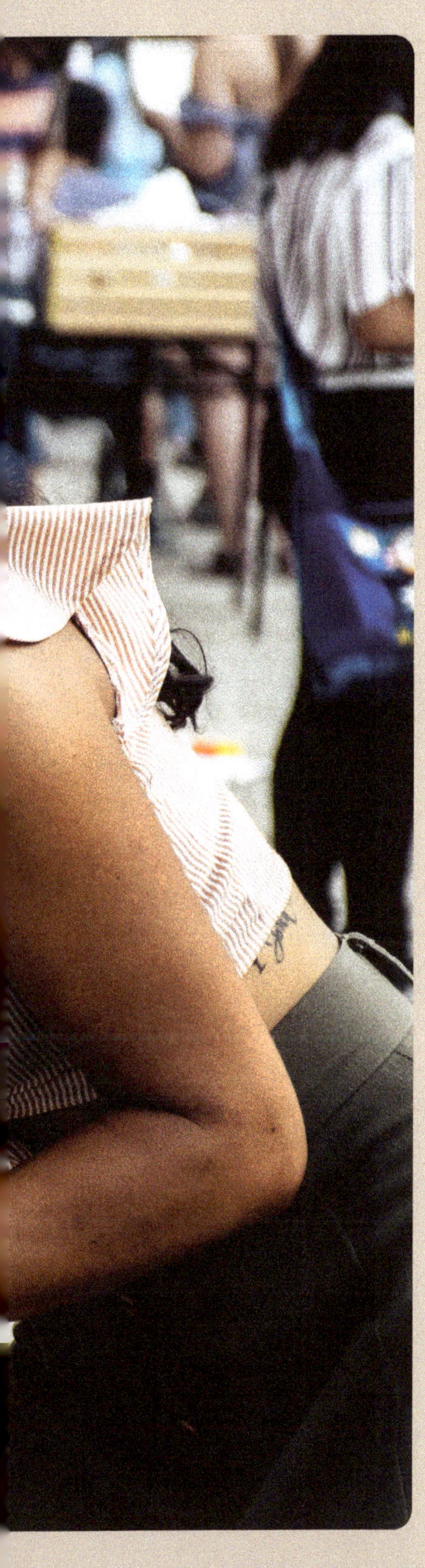

PRACTICE

The next section is all about putting the Failure Friendly mindset into practice.

The following exercise is my secret weapon for overcoming the fear of failure. It's designed to quickly get to the root of and the remedy for the fear.

This process combines every element of the Failure Friendly Mindset.

- Self-awareness with the use of non-judgemental inquiry questions
- Self-belief with positive reframing of thoughts with focus on action taking
- Self-compassion with the use of grounding breath, self-validation, body scanning and soothing

I can't wait to share it with you, so flip the flipping page, and let's get started.

Triage Your Worries

(Three questions to calm your farm)

I recorded a podcast to explain this potent practice. When you've got 20 minutes, have a listen by scanning the QR code or head to:

failurefriendly.com/triage

1 is this worry REAL?

(validation)

YES (if you feel it, it's real.)

2 is this worry TRUE?

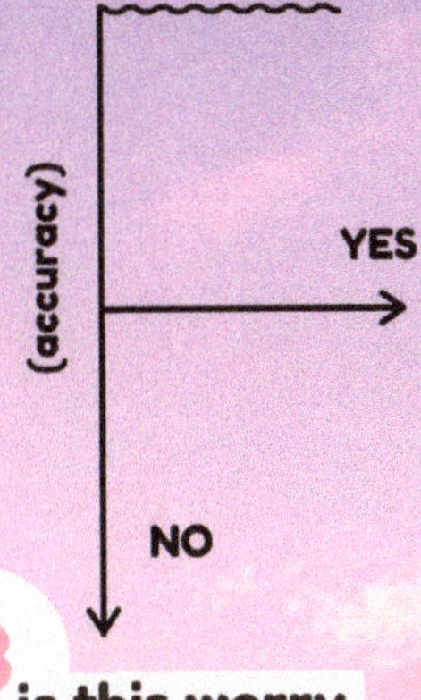

LEVEL 1: ACTION NOW

- The threat is real.
- TAKE URGENT ACTION.
  i.e. remove yourself from the situation or ask someone you trust for help.

3 is this worry HELPFUL?

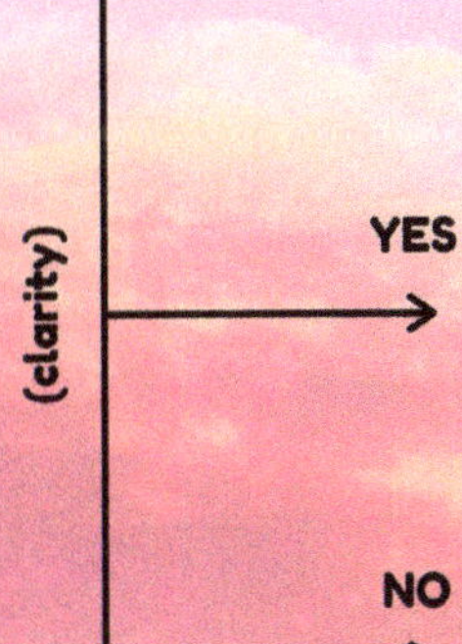

LEVEL 2: ACTION SOON

- No immediate danger but this worry is alerting you to something that could become a threat in the future.
- Turn your worry into action by finding the solution to the problem.
- Make a plan to avoid or minimise the threat.

LEVEL 3: NO ACTION

- Believing in and acting on this fear will only lead to further suffering.
- This is a growth opportunity.
- To end the vicious cycle try:
  - REFRAMING the fear with a Growth Mindset exercise.
  - RELIEVING the fear with a Self Compassion exercise.

TRIAGE YOUR WORRIES

STEP 1. Is the worry real?

The answer to this question is always 'yes'. Fear is a very real sensation. It might feel like a tight chest, butterflies in our stomach, sweaty or shaky limbs or a subtle resistance. However it expresses itself, it's a message from the body that we're in danger. Like the fear that comes with the blank page at the start of a project, the danger may not be real, but the fear definitely is.

It's important to validate your fear when you notice it and acknowledge that it's real. Fear's job is to sound the alarm that keeps us safe from danger and uncertainty. When we try to dismiss or snooze our fear response, the alarm only gets louder.

So, put a hand on your heart and take at least one deep breath to signal to your fear 'I hear you'.

By taking a moment to acknowledge the fear and validate ourselves, our bodies know we've received the message and will begin to calm down. Calming down gives us the mental clarity we need to proceed. This can be done by placing a hand on your heart, taking a deep breath and offering yourself a kind word.

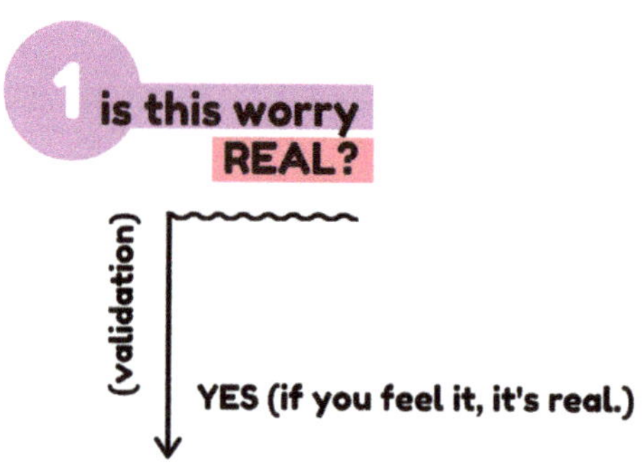

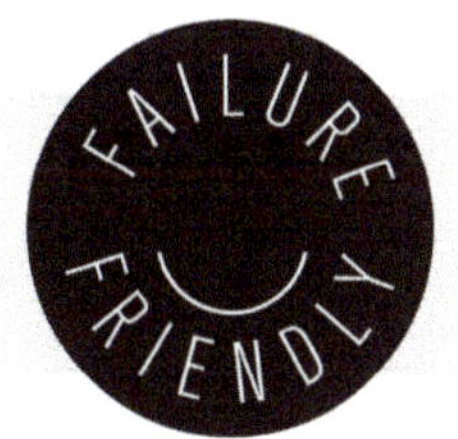

STEP 2. Is the worry true: YES (LEVEL 1 ACT NOW)

Some fears are true, such as the fear that the sound of skidding tires sends through our bodies to alert us to a true threat of danger. In those circumstances we must act immediately to remove ourselves from harm's way.

If your fear is alerting you to legit danger—something that threatens your physical or emotional safety—you must act immediately. No explanation or justification necessary; just get yourself out of there or ask someone you trust for help.

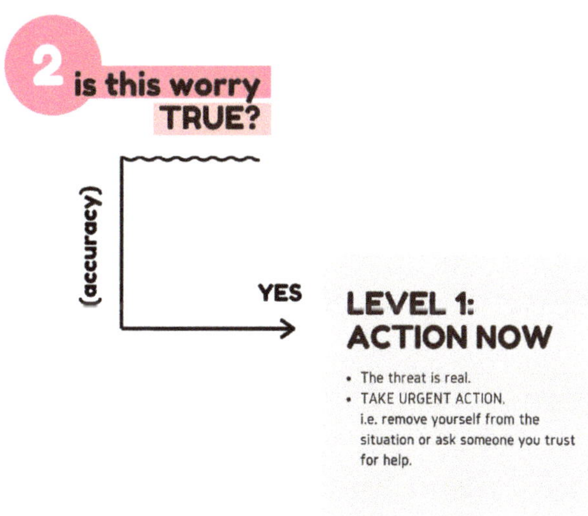

TRIAGE YOUR WORRIES

STEP 2. Is the worry helpful: NO

Most of the fears that pop into our minds are not true. Like the voice that tells us we're going to die if our next project is a flop. Not true! In a state of heightened fear, it can be hard to tell if your mind is playing tricks on you. Here's what to do: take a deep breath and ask your body, 'Is this fear real?'

If what comes up is more uncertainty, more excuses, stories and nervous mental chatter, the answer is 'No, not real'. Mental chatter is a sign that you're thinking for the answer when the goal is to feel into the question.

When you feel into a question, the answer will come from your body (or your gut). An expansive and excited feeling is a 'yes', while a constructive or dull feeling is a 'no'.

If your fear is based on an assumption, and you need more information to be sure, the answer for now is also 'No'. You will get the clarity you need in the next question. When in doubt, the answer is always 'no'.

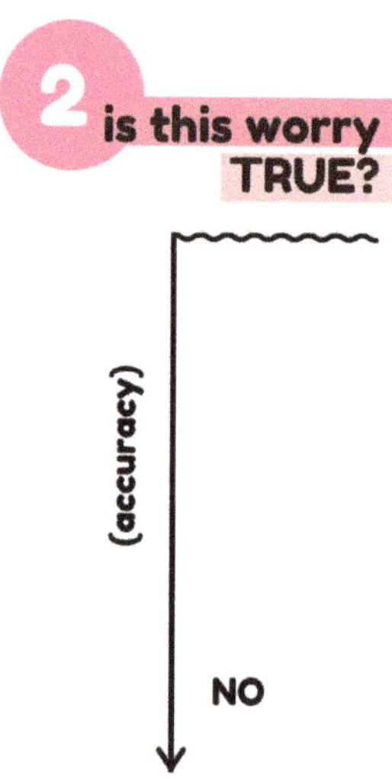

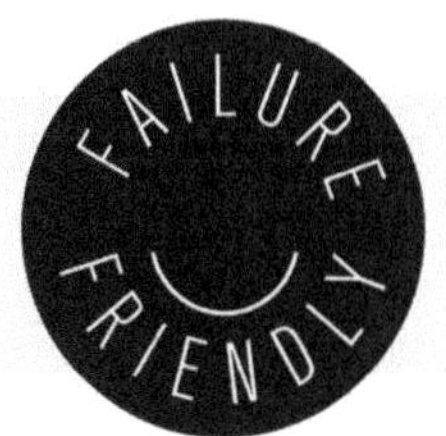

STEP 3. Is the worry helpful: YES (LEVEL 2 ACT SOON)

Just because a fear isn't true does not mean it's not useful. Many of our ridiculous fears contain information that we can use to make our lives better.

If we're anxious about doing poorly on an assignment, we can use that fear to see the importance of planning, creating a strategy, setting aside time to work on it, doing some research or asking for help. The key is take your mind out of the worst-case scenario by turning the worry into simple action steps. The smaller the steps, the better.

These worries are usually alerting us to something that could become a threat in the future and also the action we can take in the present moment to avoid or minimise the future worst-case scenario. It's not action that needs to be done immediately, as with a true fear, but it is something we need to decide to act on.

We often get anxious about things we care about or deeply want to do, so these helpful fears can guide us toward our most exciting and fulfilling lives.

TRIAGE YOUR WORRIES

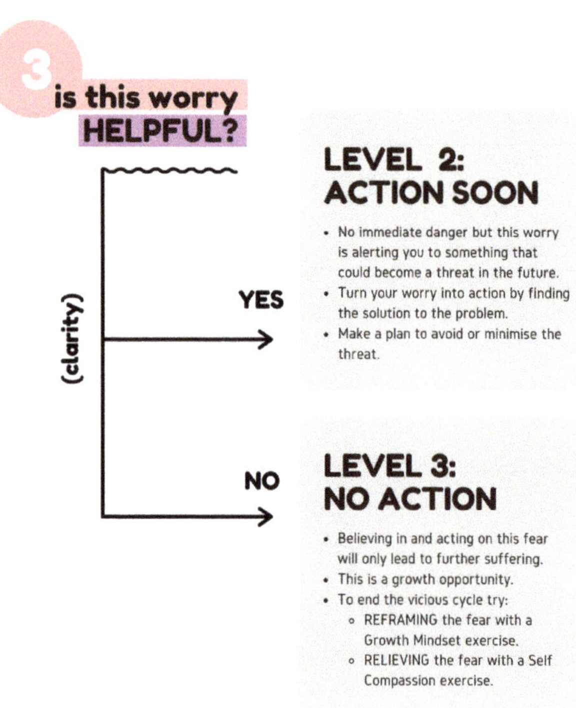

STEP 3. Is the worry helpful: NO (LEVEL 3 NO ACTION)

If you take another deep breath, put a hand on your heart and ask yourself, 'Is this worry helpful', what comes up? The moment before the answer surfaces can be an excruciating wait, but keep breathing because the answer is coming.

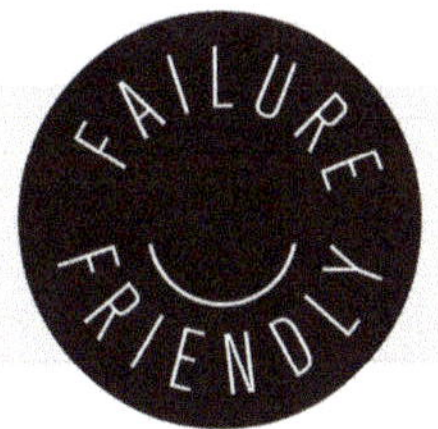

If the answer is no, the fear is not pointing you toward clear helpful action, it's instead telling you that everything is hopeless, then what you have, my friend, is not a fear at all. You have a limiting belief.

Limiting beliefs are false beliefs held in our subconscious about our abilities and the world around us, thoughts like 'I'll never be good enough' or 'nothing ever works out for me'. This is a belief that is holding you back and stopping you from seeing the awesome possibilities before you.

Nothing is ever really fixed or permanent, so if your fear is speaking to you in absolute terms like 'always' or 'never', it's telling you a lie. Continuing to believe in this fear will only lead you to further suffering, so whatever you do, don't act on this belief! Just don't!

Within these false fears are huge growth opportunities. When we face our limiting beliefs, we find a gateway to greater maturity, wisdom and freedom. Welcome to your initiation!

Transcending our limiting beliefs is not for the faint hearted. If you're ready to face your demons, here is your bonus question:

Is your limiting belief telling you that there is something wrong with you, that you are the problem? Or is it telling you there is something wrong outside of you, that the situation is hopeless or an external person is to blame?

Please ask your limiting belief 'What's the problem here? Is it me or it/them?' By pinpointing if the perceived issue is internal or external, you will find the right course of action.

TRIAGE YOUR WORRIES

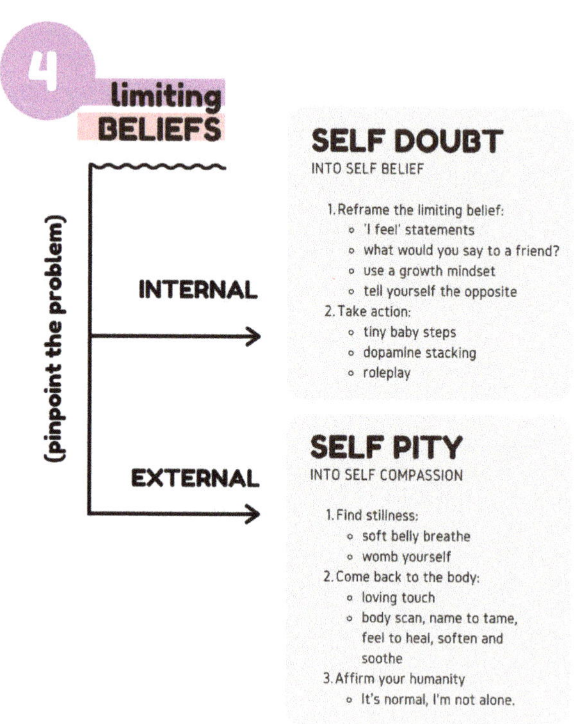

BONUS STEP. The problem is internal (SELF DOUBT)

The problem is you. Ouch. Remember, this is a limiting belief, meaning it's not true. It's limiting you and keeping you stuck because your brain is working with faulty information. Accurate thinking does not keep us stuck. When we've pinpointed the true cause and effect, solutions begin to produce themselves naturally. If no solutions are in sight, and you feel stuck, this is a sign that your mind is working with a lie.

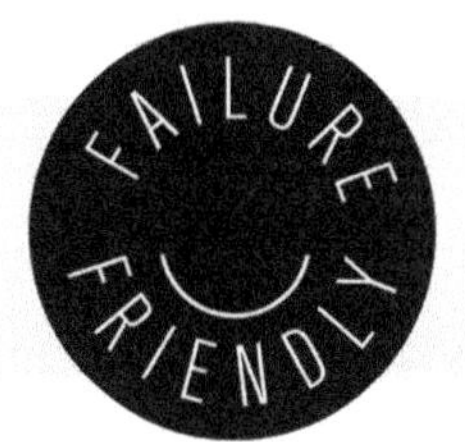

The truth is: your emotions, achievements and failures are just life experiences. They don't change the fact that you are perfectly human.

When you are experiencing self-doubt, the limiting belief can be so deeply ingrained that you can't just shake it off. You've believed it for so long that a part of you wants it to be true. Ideas you've held for years or decades don't suddenly fall away the moment you wake up to them. It's a process of rewiring your brain. This is where you move from triaging your worries to actually treating them. Beginners to the Failure Friendly Mindset will find listening to their thoughts challenging enough. When you feel safe and ready to go a step further, here are my tips for rewiring the self-doubting mind.

First, swap self-doubt for self-belief by shaking up your self-talk. This is called 'reframing'. You can do this by:

- Using 'I feel' statements. Rather than 'I am helpless', try 'I feel helpless', or better yet, 'I currently feel helpless, but this will pass'. By distancing ourselves from the painful emotion, we allow it to be what it is, a temporary experience. Remember: doubt is normal. Self-doubt is dangerous.
- Ask yourself, 'What would I say to a friend in the same situation?' This will remove your personal bias and help you see the full picture.
- Reframe using a growth mindset. Instead of 'I can't', try 'I can't yet'.
- Try telling yourself the exact opposite. (This is my favourite!)

TRIAGE YOUR WORRIES

Behind all of my limiting thoughts was the belief 'I can't'. When I started reframing my self-talk with the opposite thought, 'I can', my challenges didn't suddenly shift, but something did. The limiting belief was born from a twisted logic that said, 'Well, I'm in pain. I must deserve it'. So, when I gave myself encouragement instead of criticism, the same logic said, 'Well, I'm being treated well, I must deserve it.' This began the unravelling of the old thinking.

The fastest way to change our thinking is by changing our behaviour, which is why the second tip is taking action.

The thing that your mind is saying can't do, that's what you've got to do here. It's called 'faking it till you make it' or 'feeling fear and doing it anyway'. The secret to doing the impossible is:

- Breaking the task into tiny, tiny baby steps. Instead of focusing on the end goal or the to-do list, focus on the next tiny step. If the goal is to write a song, your tiny step might be finding a pen, cleaning your instrument, or taking a deep breath. The steps need to be so tiny that they seem unrelated to the goal.

- Focus on one tiny action at a time. Talk yourself through each action, 'I am opening the door', 'I am walking, left foot, right foot'. If you notice yourself in reflection mode and adding commentary and judgment, hone your focus back to the action and nothing else.

- Celebrate each tiny step you take. This is non-negotiable. Each time you acknowledge your effort, you trigger a dopamine hit in your brain. Dopamine is rocket fuel for the mind. This is also called 'dopamine stacking'. It can be as simple as crossing a task off the list, or you can physically pat yourself on the back. When you do devalue your

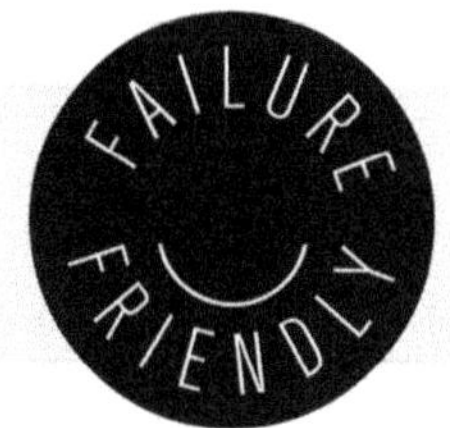

efforts, you must celebrate twice to make up for it. Celebrate the thing you accidentally devalued, and then celebrate the act of catching and correcting yourself.

- One thing at a time. A brain that is trying to overcome habitual self-doubt is easily overwhelmed. Long to-do lists are overwhelming because your brain begins to worry about each task at once. Help your brain separate the steps from the end product by putting your to-do list away.

- Be playful. Check out the warm up and learning activities listed in the resources section for role-playing ideas that make action taking fun.

Q. How is finding a pen really going to help me write a song?

A. The thing about tiny, tiny baby steps is that they create momentum, and that's how we get unstuck. Once we've built momentum by ticking off these tiny tasks, it's much harder to give up, and those scary 'limitations' don't feel so impossible when we're approaching them at speed.

Start shaking up your self-doubt by referring back to the Shake Up action card activities, or try the worksheet activities in the resources section (the Face, Flip & Free worksheet and the Reframing Guide would be perfect).

TRIAGE YOUR WORRIES

BONUS STEP. The problem is external (SELF PITY)

The problem is outside of you. There's nothing you can do. You're the helpless victim. Or so it seems. Remember, this is a limiting belief, meaning it's not true.

When you are experiencing self-pity, the limiting belief can be so deeply ingrained that you can't just release it. It has literally brainwashed you to believe you don't have the power to. Rewiring this belief is a process. Are you ready? When you feel safe and ready to go a step further, here are my tips for dissolving self-pity.

First, swap self-pity for self-compassion by finding stillness. Just because we are frozen and stuck does not mean we are still. Stillness is a healthy expression of feminine energy. It has a calm, womblike quality that allows energy to move through it. You can achieve this by:

- 'Wombing' yourself - Get comfortable, wrap yourself in a fuzzy blanket, or slip into a warm bath or hot shower. Let yourself feel held and safe.
- Still your mind by slowing your breath - Breathe as slowly and quietly as you can for at least three breaths. Use a straw if you have one. Let your belly go soft, and feel it expand like a balloon as you breathe deeply.
- A purposeful cuppa - Or any self-care activity that feels good. Just allow yourself to do it purposefully. Everything paused, no multitasking, no scrolling, no worrying, just you and this moment. It's yours.
- Charge your space - This is a woo-woo way of saying clean up, declutter, deep clean, light a candle or just move things around until it feels better.

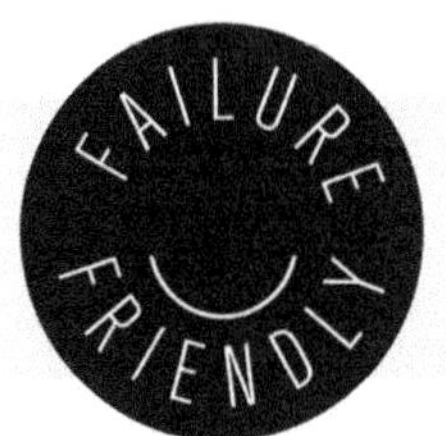

- Release stagnant energy with gentle movement - Roll your shoulders, do a slow yoga flow or freestyle some tai chi moves in flowing attire.
- Step into nature - Connect with Mother Earth's energy by watching waves crash on the sand or clouds float in the sky. Feel the wind on your face, listen for birdsong or smell the flowers. Just show up and let nature disarm your senses with its beauty.
- Settle and rebalance your nervous system - Search YouTube for vagus nerve exercises to get out of fight-or-flight mode and release stress from the body.

The mind processes our thoughts, the body processes our feelings.

When I really surrender to stillness, something amazing happens. In this state I'm suddenly allowed to feel whatever I'm feeling. Nothing is wrong, and nothing needs fixing. Anxiety becomes a sensation in my body rather than a war inside my mind. I can allow and observe it. It's an uncomfortable sensation but not unbearable. As I let it be, it begins to move and change, becoming more intense and less intense, and then it's gone. I'm left feeling different. I feel cleansed and renewed, stronger and wiser. Healed. It's not magic; it's what the body is designed to do. While the mind processes our thoughts, the body processes our feelings.

TRIAGE YOUR WORRIES

This brings me to the second way to turn self-pity into self-compassion by coming back to the body. Self-pity often comes with feeling numb and disconnected. Here are my tips for reconnecting:

- Loving touch - Put your hand over your heart and hold yourself. With loving kindness coax the discomfort away from your mind and into your heart and body. Then try rubbing your heart space in a slow, circular motion. Methods like EFT tapping and self-massage with oils or moisturisers are also very effective.
- Body scan - Scanning from the tips of your toes to the top of your head, pay attention to all of your body parts and bodily sensations, noticing where you are holding aches, tension or areas of relaxation. Curiosity is key.
- Name it to tame it - After scanning, identify what the sensation is. Which emotion does it feel like? Speak it out loud. For example, 'I feel fear in the pit of my stomach'.
- Feel it to heal it - Now that you know what the sensation is and where, spend some time allowing it to be there and feeling it. If this becomes too intense, return to your breath.
- Soften, soothe and allow - Send your breath and healing intention to the discomfort. Visualise the edges of the discomfort softening.
- Dance or shake the numbness away.

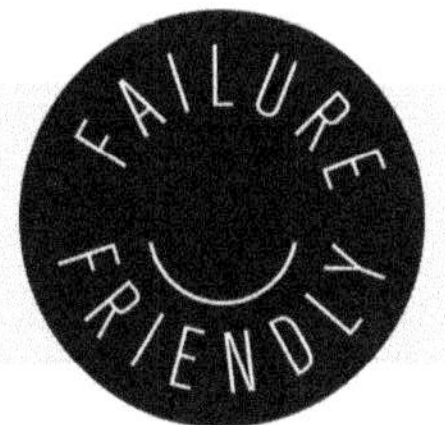

Self-compassion is all about feeling emotions and trusting the mystery of the process, even when we don't have all the answers (especially when you don't have all the answers).

When we feel an uncomfortable emotion, we can sometimes jump into fixing mode. With good intentions we want to pinpoint the problem, so we can solve it, pronto. We do this by asking ourselves 'Why?' or 'What's wrong?'

The '5 Whys' activity is one of my favourite Shake Up exercises for reframing self-doubt. It helps us discover the limiting belief behind the mental chatter. But emotions are not the same as mental chatter.

When we've been triggered into a heightened state, we rarely have the mental clarity to know what or why we're triggered. We can't answer the question, and the added uncertainty of where these intense emotions are coming from escalates the situation. The perceived unpredictability of our own feelings leads to us to feel out of control and unsafe.

It's only once we have soothed ourselves that we can reflect on the situation to see the cause and effect. This is why the first step in the 'Triaging Your Worries' practice is validation. Being allowed to feel the way you do, no questions asked and no matter how 'silly' it may seem, is what self-compassion is all about.

Instead of asking 'Why?', ask 'What do I need?' Or better yet just allow yourself to express the feeling. When we accept ourselves in all our emotional states, meeting our negativity with the same respect we show our positivity, it reinforces to our subconscious that we are unconditionally supported. This unconditional acceptance is what makes us feel safe and gives us the strength to weather the storms of uncertainty.

TRIAGE YOUR WORRIES

Shame will tell us to hide our pain and not share our flaws because it will expose that we are different and wrong. The opposite is actually true. By being vulnerable with ourselves and welcoming our pain rather than turning away from it, we remember that pain and discomfort are not different and wrong; they are a normal part of human life. We are simply experiencing things that all humans have to deal with.

Normalising pain takes the edge off our suffering because remembering we are human also reminds us we are part of something much bigger: humanity. Suddenly, we are not alone in our darkness because everybody feels this way from time to time. We share this experience with everyone who's been there before and everyone who will be there again. We deserve compassion not because we are good but merely because we are human.

Self compassion connects us to our human-ness and our humanity.

This moment of connection with the greater whole or 'oneness', as the yogis call it, helps us to settle into the mystery of life. Instead of feeling separate, we can feel included, supported and safe in the unfolding process.

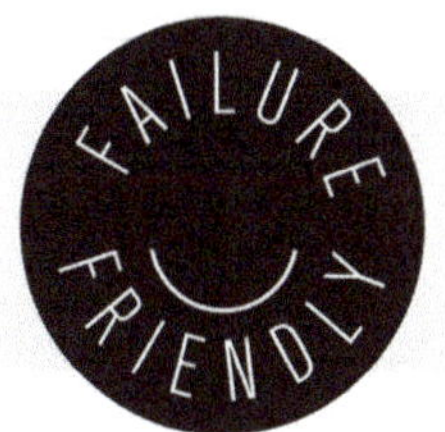

This is why my third and final tip for dissolving self-pity is to connect to your human-ness and greater humanity. Here are my tips for tapping into oneness.

Soothe Yourself with Inclusive Self-Compassion Affirmations:

- This is normal, and I am not alone in this. We're in the struggle together.
- Everyone feels this way from time to time.
- This pain is part of the human condition. It's a part of life (and it sucks, but that's okay).
- I'm not the first to experience something like this, and I won't be the last.
- It's okay to feel this way. It's okay.
- Creative life is supposed to be challengeing and humans are designed to do hard things. I've done hard things before, I will get through this.
- It's part of the process, it's all part of the process.
- May I be safe, may I be happy and may I be free from pain.
- May we be safe, may we be happy and may we be free from pain.

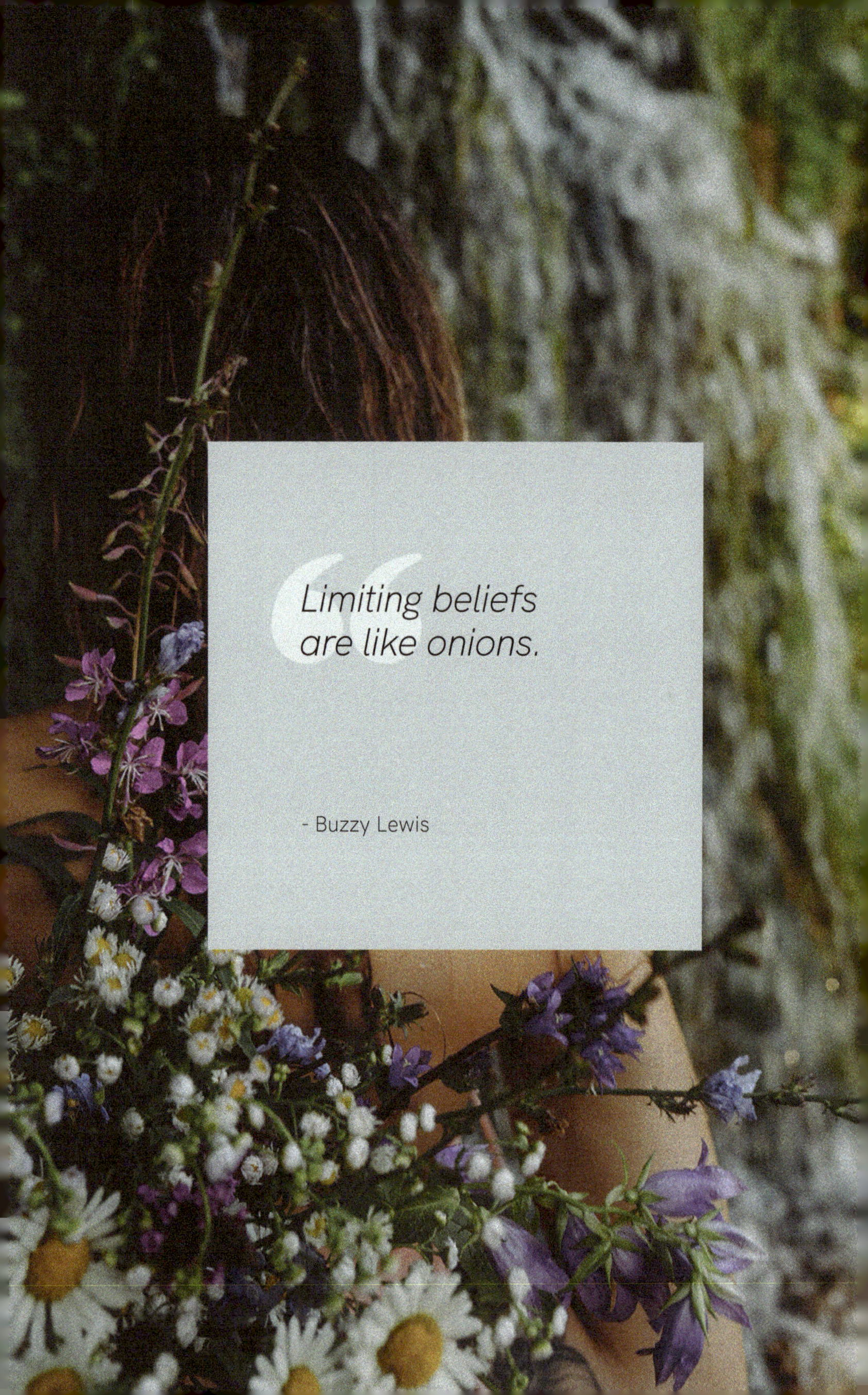
Limiting beliefs
are like onions.
- Buzzy Lewis

THE DEEP WORK

Limiting beliefs are like onions. Every time we practice reframing, positive action, stillness, being in our bodies and connecting to oneness, we unravel our limiting beliefs to reveal another layer of conditioning.

It's an almost daily practice and a lifelong process of journeying layer by layer to deeper and deeper healing. It keeps life interesting.

If you would rather avoid the repetition and just slice your way straight to the core of the psychological onion, know that it is possible but it's not easy. Like a real onion, it also involves many tears.

This deep healing work requires the highest level of emotional maturity. That is why my tips for deep healing are for mature readers only.

To receive a copy of my recommendations for deep healing, you can reach out to me on Instagram (@failure_friendly)
or on email (buzzy@failurefriendly.com).

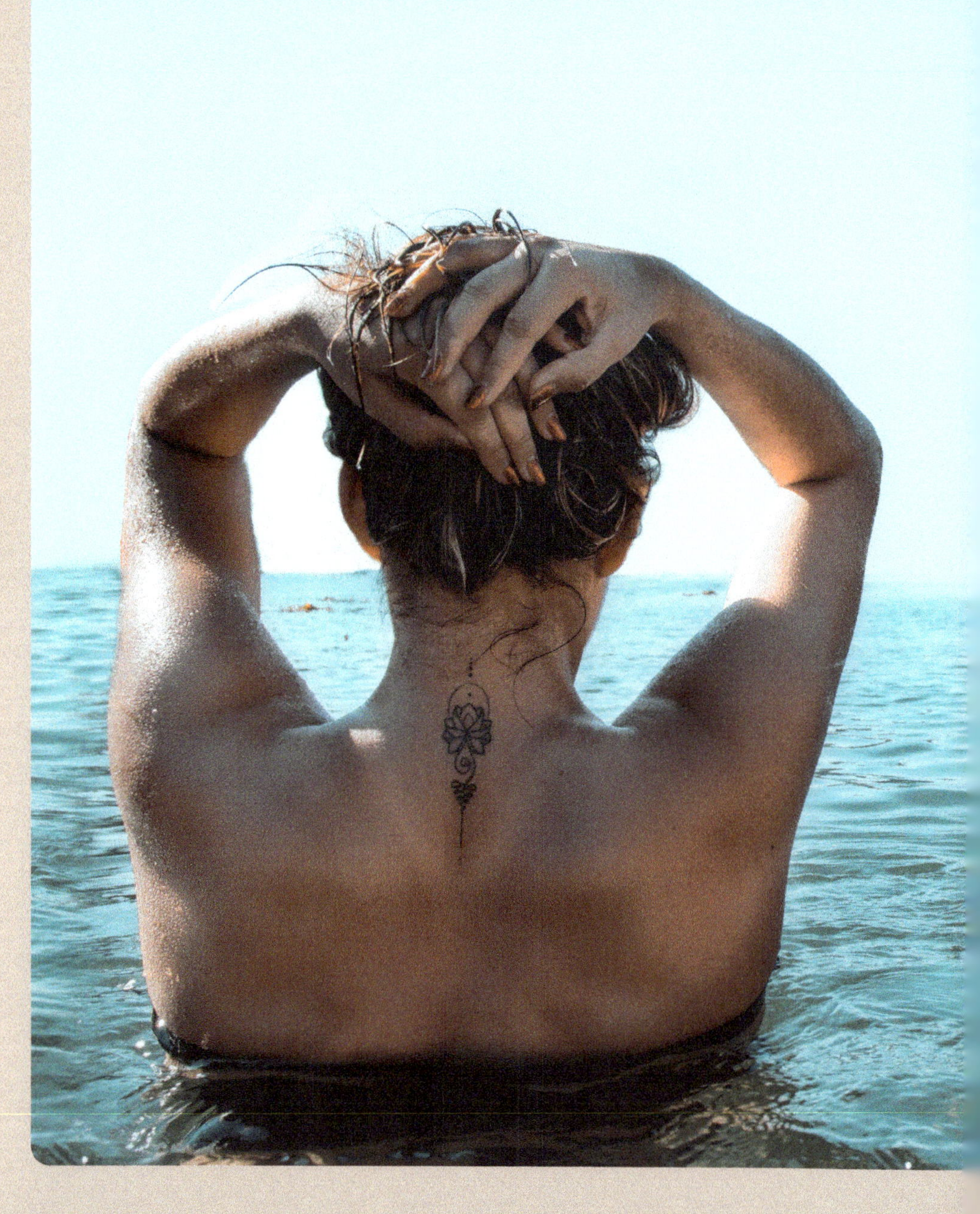

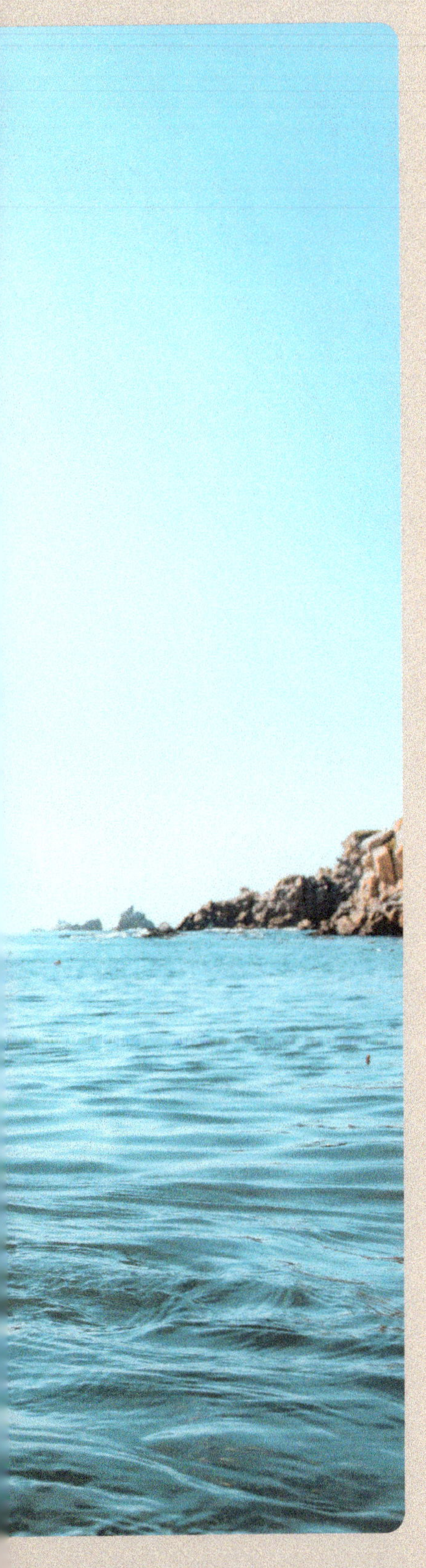

EXPERIENCE

Now that you've set the foundations, learned the skills and put it all into practice, next is the lived experience.

When you begin to trust yourself and the process, the practice becomes less about mindset tools or exercises and more about energetics and intuition.

In this next section I've outlined some of the exciting yet subtle shifts that can be experienced when you embrace a Failure Friendly way of life. I have tried to put into words what this sense of inner harmony looks like on a practical level and how you can start achieving it for yourself.

STAYING BALANCED

Opposites attract

Everywhere we look we can see a balancing act of opposite forces. For example, there is a constant swing from day to night, from summer to winter, fallow to fertile and the list goes on. It's the continuous rhythm from one extreme to another that keeps everything balanced.

If you're feeling off, think about your current energetic state and how you can shift into the opposite energy state. When we feel cold, we naturally find the opposite of cold by seeking warmth. Just as it would be silly to feel cold and then look for ways to get cooler, it is silly to feel a negative emotion and then seek out more negativity.

Instead of giving your fear more fear or adding shame and anger to the situation, look instead for the opposite state of fear. Loving kindness and positivity rebalances us when we fall into fear.

If tough love is your vibe, then 'you do you'. But if you want the fastest way to move through the obstacles that come with creative work, I urge you to try on this paradoxical approach. Whenever you feel off, use the following self-awareness check-in to remedy the situation.

Imagine a spectrum of energy. On the far left is our healthy masculine energy, which fades from clear action-taking into unhealthy and anxious action that burnouts into 'no energy' in the middle. From there the energy shifts into unhealthy feminine energy that's lethargic and depressive, then it grows into healthy feminine energy with compassionate flow on the far right. Check in with your energy to see where you are on the spectrum.

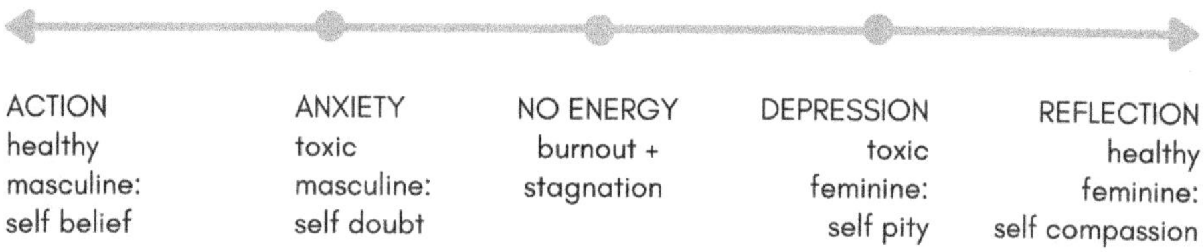

ACTION	ANXIETY	NO ENERGY	DEPRESSION	REFLECTION
healthy masculine: self belief	toxic masculine: self doubt	burnout + stagnation	toxic feminine: self pity	healthy feminine: self compassion

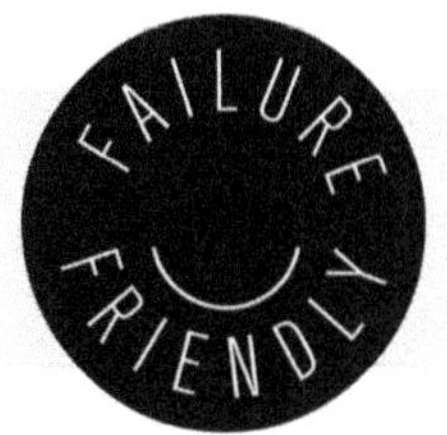

If you feel you're spun yourself into an anxious frenzy, addicted to the buzz and unable to stop, you likely have an excess of masculine action-taking energy. To rebalance yourself go to the opposite side of the spectrum. Try some opposing feminine energy exercises with the suggested MAKE UP card activities.

If you feel you've fallen into a depressed slump, dwelling on problems and licking your wounds, you likely have an excess of feminine reflective energy. To rebalance yourself go to the opposite side of the spectrum. Try some opposing masculine energy exercises with the suggested SHAKE UP card activities.

Q. Does this mean we should also respond to positivity with negativity?

A. We only need to rebalance ourselves when we feel off balance. Feeling consumed with fear is a sign that we have already added fear to fear or negativity to negativity and disturbed the natural balance. The discomfort is a sign that we need to add positivity to the negativity. Yes, there can be times when we need to add negativity to positivity. Sometimes we can use positivity to shield ourselves from our true emotions, which eventually wears us down. When we feel exhausted by the 'happy act', this discomfort is a sign that we need to acknowledge and feel the negative emotions. But if you're feeling fine and in the flow of positivity, there is no need to seek out negativity. Listen to your body.

STAYING BALANCED

The Middle
Let's talk about the middle of the spectrum, the dreaded point of 'no energy'. This is the void between masculine and feminine energy. You can find yourself immobilised here when you take too much action and not enough rest, or when you take too much rest and not enough action. You can also end up here because of an experience of grief, of trauma, of being in crisis or getting sick.

In the void, without our usual level of energy, we stop feeling alive and human. It's a lot of sitting and staring. In this state, 'Shake Up' and 'Make Up' exercises can't help us because there's no masculine or feminine energy to call on, there isn't any energy at all.

In the void state time loses meaning, it simultaneously stands still and whirls passed. It can feel like we've been stuck in the rut for an eternity and there's no end in sight. Feeling trapped in this in-between is incredibly distressing. And the distress gets worse when we pressure or shame ourselves to bust out of there already!

There are two important things to know about the void. The first, is that it's a temporary experience (meaning you won't be stuck there forever). And the second, is that it's a useful and normal experience* (not an epic failure).

Your energy will always come back, because in life, the only constant is change. Even though you can't snap your fingers and turn your energy back on, it doesn't mean it won't suddenly shift, it will. When it will come back is the mystery, but it will be sooner than you think.

The void is not the trap, thinking is. In the void we don't have the energy to do anything else but think, so it's easy to fall into overthinking. Like we discovered on page 17, while thinking helps us feel in control and safe, all it really does is reinforce the false belief that we can't trust ourselves and the process.

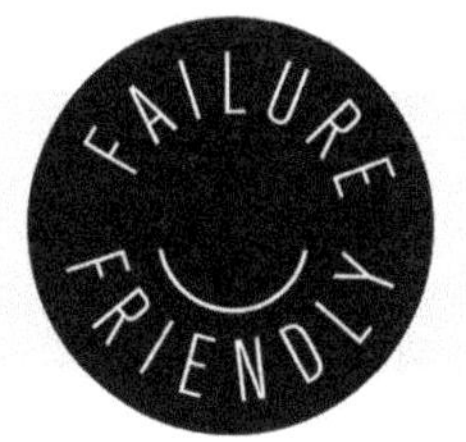

Instead of spiralling into fearful thoughts, try casting your mind forward. I like to ask myself 'will I even remember this in five years?' or 'will I still care about this experience in five months?' By giving your mind an end point to focus on helps it to contain the uncertainty. Imagining just for a second a future free from suffering gives our mind a breather. By zooming out we create a moment of self-awareness.

Self-awareness is the key to surviving the void and potentially enjoying it. The Failure Friendly 'Wake Up' activities help us become non-judgmental observers of our thoughts and experience. This allows us to stop worrying and problem solving and just accept the moment as it is. This point of acceptance, like we learnt on page 21, is when the process starts to get fun.

When we accept that we are in the void and there's nothing for us to do but ride it out, we can soften towards it and ourselves, and begin to embrace the benefits. The void is a hard reset. Just like our electronic devices that sometimes need to shut down completely for ten seconds before turning them back on. We too need to take time to reboot. The void state is purifying and restorative. Our body knows what it's doing, even if we don't, and leaning into its mysterious intelligence is kind of magical. To be honest, it's a relief not to be in control all the time.

I used to think the end goal of working with the energy spectrum was to avoid the void space. While my aim is still to flow rhythmically between action and reflection, I now appreciate that the occasional hard reset is part of being human. If I find myself in the middle, the space between energies, I try not to despair. Because after my zombie trance or monk-like meditation, my energy will come back with the bonus of renewed gratitude and lust for life.

**If you are experiencing the void state more often than not, it's a good idea to check in with a mental health professional. You deserve to feel good the majority of the time.*

STAYING BALANCED

Riding the wave

Once you start dipping into masculine action when you're drowning in feminine reflection and vice versa, you'll begin to appreciate the wave.

The wave represents the interrelated connection between the two energies. You'll begin to see that rest and reflection are that much more satisfying and easier to tap into after you've exerted yourself with challenging action, and that challenging action is so much more precise and powerful when you're well rested and focussed from contemplation. Each energy fuels the other.

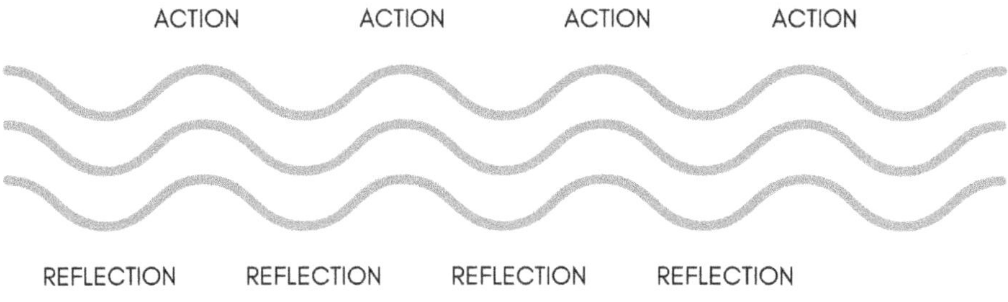

Rather than waiting to shift gears when you feel off balance, proactively design your day, week or month around the wave. If you have an action-heavy morning, schedule in more reflective activities soon after and then something challenging after that. On and on it goes, up and down, creating a perfect rhythm.

Self-doubt and self-pity disconnect us from our intuition or gut feelings. By riding the wave of action/reflection/action/reflection and checking in to see how our energy is responding to these subtle shifts, we begin to reconnect with our own energy.

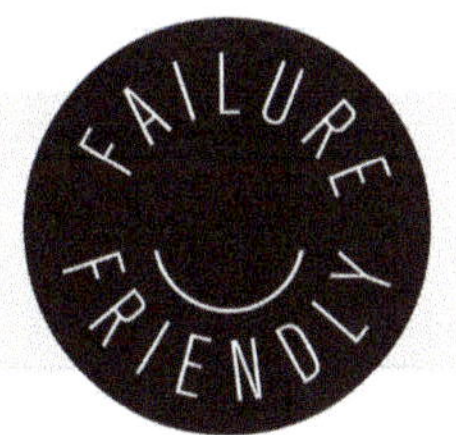

Soon you will feel your energy begin to shift. Rather than working for set times or on set tasks you'll know when it's time for you to stop or go. I was pretty excited when I began to identify a niggling discomfort that surfaces when I scroll through Instagram. Before I would have continued scrolling until I got distracted with something else. I would have fried my brain cells with content overload and finished feeling foggy or hungover. Now I know that that feeling, with its subtle shift in energy, is telling me 'That's enough. This was fun, but now it's time to exert energy, not inhale it'.

I have to force myself to get out in the garden. I used to tell myself, 'Stop when you've weeded this section'. But now, much to my surprise, I'll finish that section, and something inside me says, 'Keep going'. So, I start weeding another section. Then it begins to drizzle rain, a perfect excuse to call it a day. But my energy says, 'Not yet. Keep going'. So, I keep going for another ten minutes or so until the energy shifts, and I know I'm done. I realise then that if I had stopped sooner, I wouldn't have been able to settle and relax. There was more energy in the tank that wanted to be used.

Why am I telling you this? Because it's the simple things that make the big difference. This simple communication I have with myself is what turns an ordinary day into an extraordinary day. Trusting myself to know what I need and that the process always supports me, has allowed me to meet the uncomfortable resistance that comes with creative work with joy and kindness, rather than the panic and second-guessing that used to send me into a negative spiral.

This is where you come in. I hope you can take these lessons, make them your own and ultimately find your way back to yourself. When you clear the blocks and conditioning that tell you it's not safe to trust - you'll reconnect with your authenticity, your guiding intuition and those gut feels! They belong to you, so go get them!

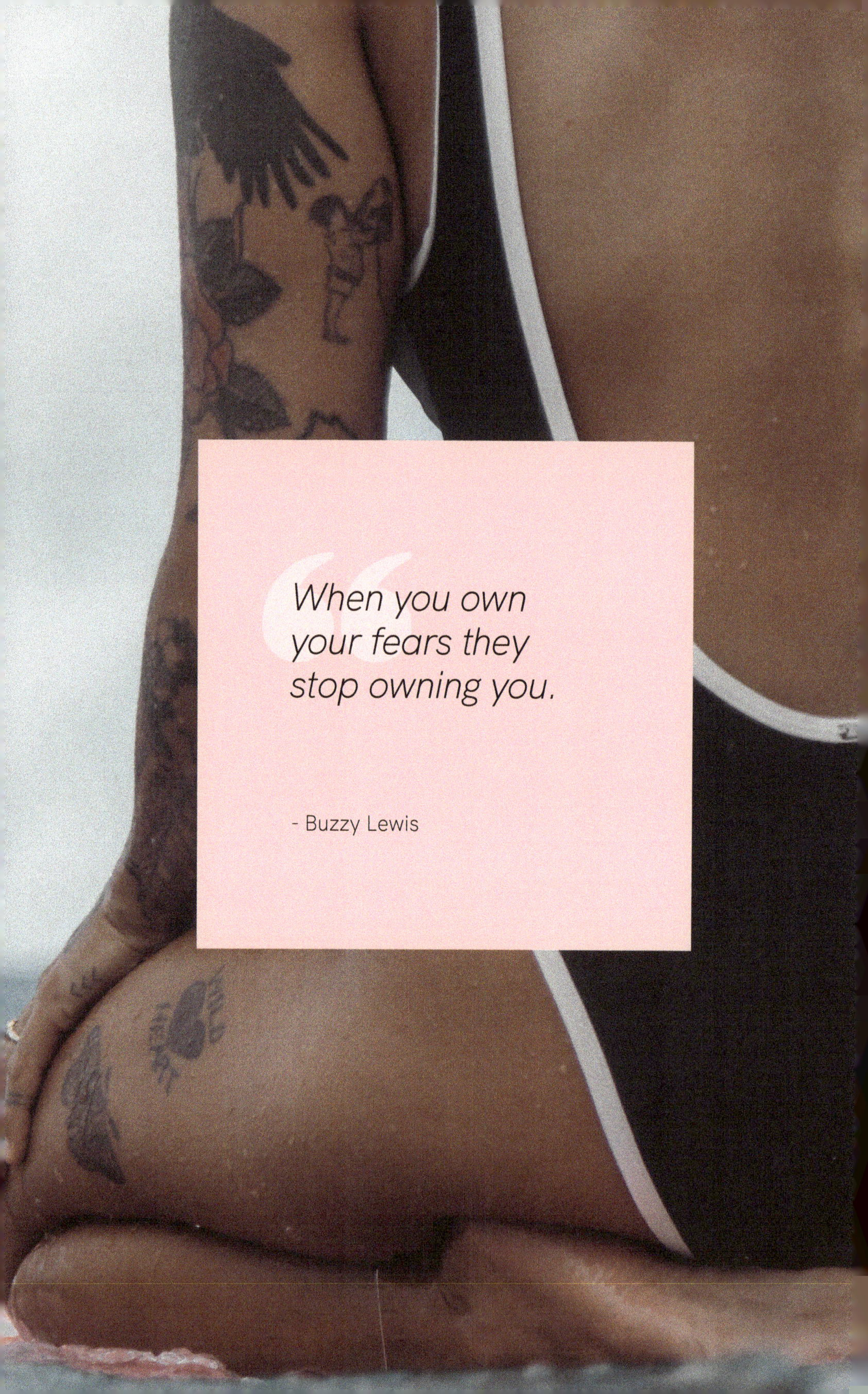
When you own
your fears they
stop owning you.
- Buzzy Lewis

REFLECTIONS

My biggest takeaway from six years of research into the fear of failure is that bravery starts with being completely honest with yourself. There have been times in my Failure Friendly journey where I felt truly unstoppable and then other times where I felt stuck and too timid to make a move.

When I look over my old journals from both periods, I see that the more unstoppable version of myself was not fearless. I had just as many fears then as my timid self, if not more. The only difference between the two was my willingness to own my fears.

The timid me stayed on the surface. I didn't dive deeper into how I was really feeling. I kept the truth locked away, even from myself. Meanwhile, the unstoppable me just laid it all out there on the table, no matter how childish or embarrassing it sounded.

When I am brave enough to admit how un-brave I'm feeling, and softly meet myself in all the places I feel weak and unsure, I give myself the power to overcome it.

MENTAL HEALTH CHECK

Validating yourself can look like:

- Starting projects easily, without too much planning
- Sharing your ideas and creative work
- Saying 'no' to tasks and invitations that don't light you up
- Cutting your losses and moving on when things don't feel right
- Not feeling a need to explain yourself and your reasoning
- Accepting compliments and praise without deflection
- Not taking criticism or praise personally
- Staying focussed on the process and detached from the results
- Taking rest without needing to earn it
- Asking for forgiveness rather than permission
- Meeting your own needs and not expecting others to do it for you
- Letting go of grudges while maintaining boundaries
- Being unproductive without feelings of guilt or shame
- Owning your mistakes and learning from them
- Being proactive instead of apologetic
- Taking time to grieve ideas that didn't work out
- Letting go of perfectionism (done is better than perfect)
- Being kind to yourself during difficult experiences
- Taking an equal role in collaborative projects
- Being patient with yourself and others
- Taking action when we feel inspired rather than ready
- Taking time to celebrate your own effort, progress and achievements
- Taking time to honour your own struggles and emotional wounds
- Checking in with your needs and wants before acting
- Valuing your own opinion
- Culling meetings, tasks and projects to focus on your priorities
- Being discerning when choosing projects and collaborators
- Acting on your gut feelings rather than logic

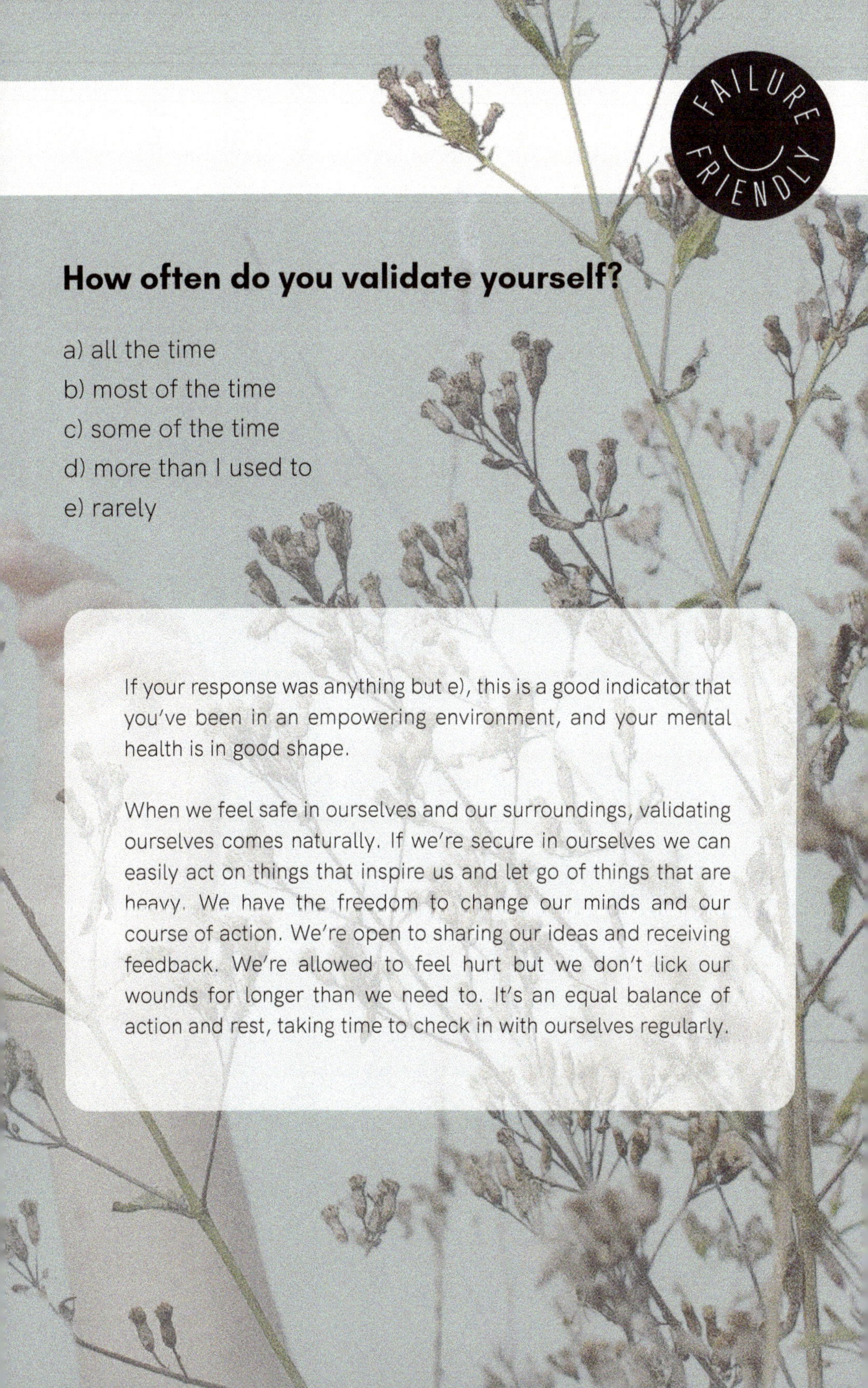

How often do you validate yourself?

a) all the time
b) most of the time
c) some of the time
d) more than I used to
e) rarely

If your response was anything but e), this is a good indicator that you've been in an empowering environment, and your mental health is in good shape.

When we feel safe in ourselves and our surroundings, validating ourselves comes naturally. If we're secure in ourselves we can easily act on things that inspire us and let go of things that are heavy. We have the freedom to change our minds and our course of action. We're open to sharing our ideas and receiving feedback. We're allowed to feel hurt but we don't lick our wounds for longer than we need to. It's an equal balance of action and rest, taking time to check in with ourselves regularly.

THE RECAP

To live a highly creative life, free from the fear of failure, you need two things:

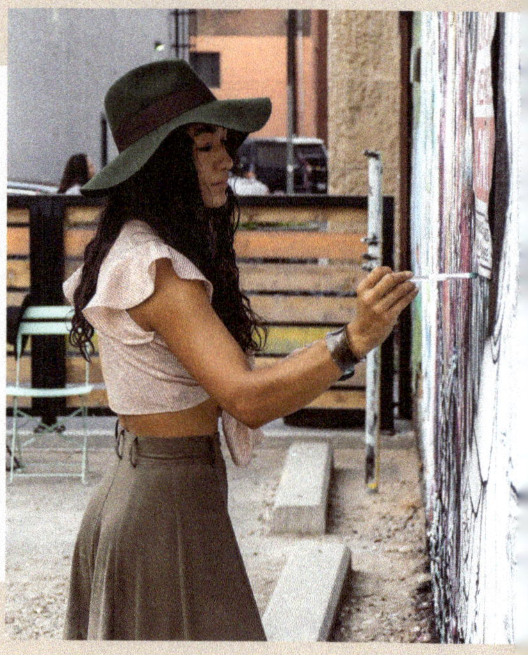

1. *An unshakable trust in yourself*
2. *An unconditional trust in the process*

This is achieved by learning the three Failure Friendly Skills:

(It is only by facing our lower or flawed self that we are able to mature and become our highest self. This means that the things you think are keeping you from success are actually the vehicles to achieve it).

WAKE UP:
turning self consciousness into self awareness

SHAKE UP:
turning self doubt into self belief

MAKE UP:
turning self pity into self compassion

Triage your worries by asking if your fears are:

REAL?

TRUE?

HELPFUL?

Transcend your limitations by asking your limiting beliefs if the problem is:

INTERNAL:
This is an experience of self-doubt that calls for self-belief exercises.

EXTERNAL:
This is an experience of self-pity that calls for self-compassion practices.

Staying balanced requires an understanding that there are two energy polarities: masculine action and feminine reflection. When we feel off balance, the trick is to engage with the opposite energy to that which we are currently experiencing.

Instead of fearing your fear, meet the fear with sweet loving kindness and positivity.

BOOK CLUB

Hungry for more? Here are some Failure Friendly authors who belong on every creative person's book shelf.

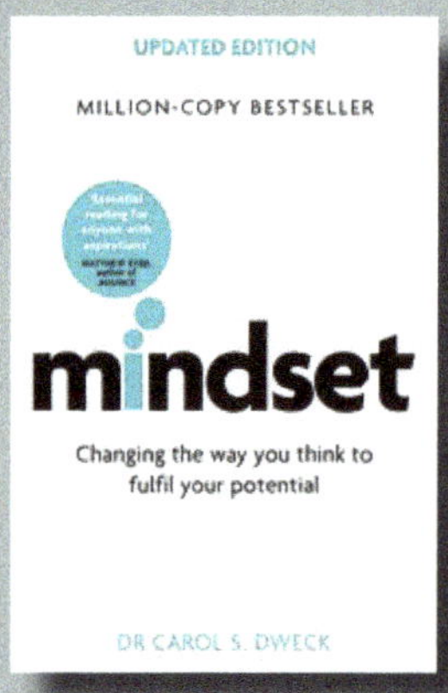

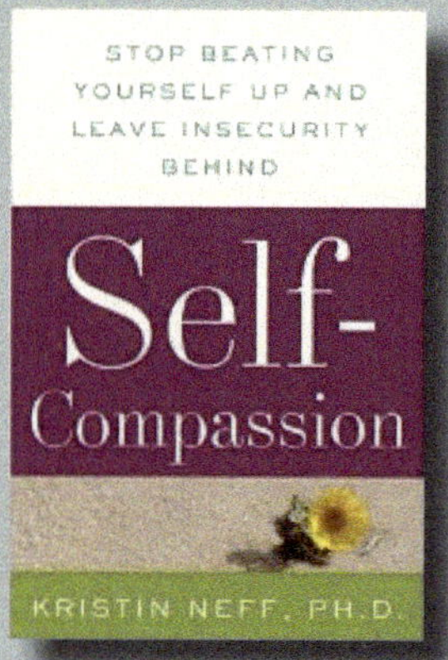

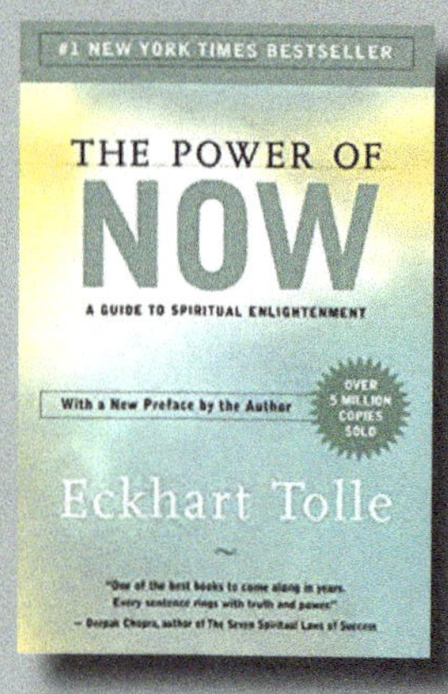

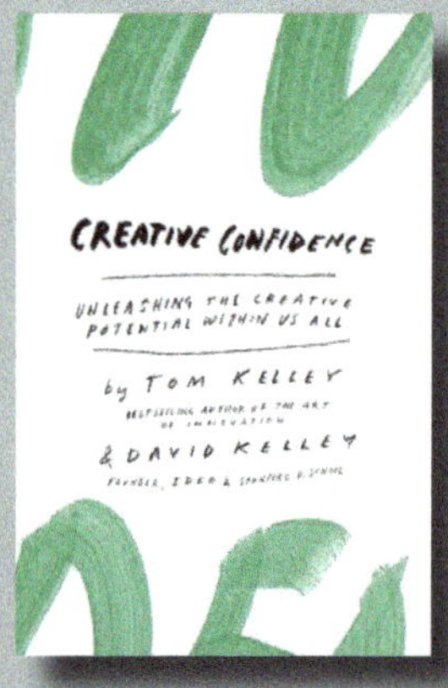

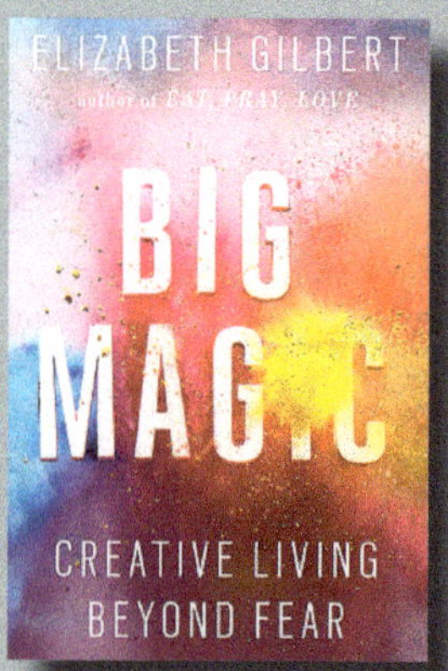

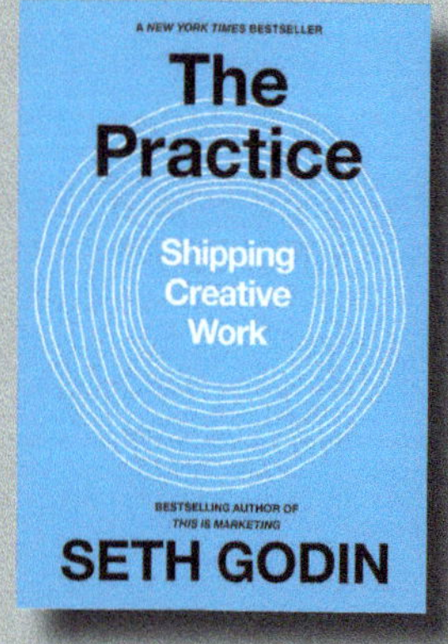

Mindset by Carol Dweck, Self-Compassion by Kristen Neff, The Power of Now by Eckhart Tolle, Creative Confidence by Tom and David Kelley, Big Magic by Elizabeth Gilbert, The Practice by Seth Godin, The Nine Modern Day Muses by Jill Badonsky, Living with a Creative Mind by Jeff and Julia Crabtree, The Desire Map by Danielle LaPorte, A Return to Love by Marianne Williamson, Goddess Wisdom by Tanishka, and The Gifts of Imperfection by Brene Brown.

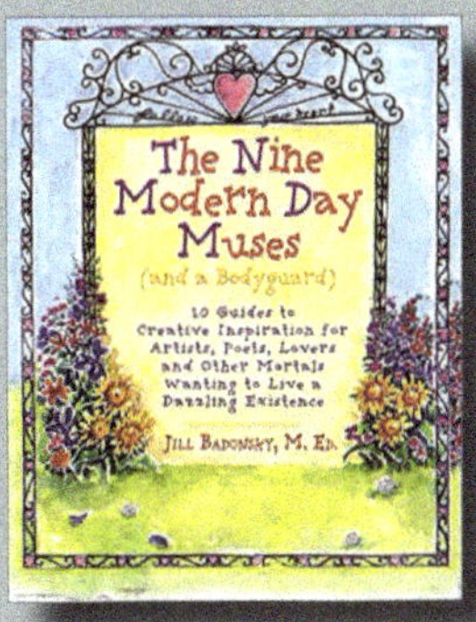

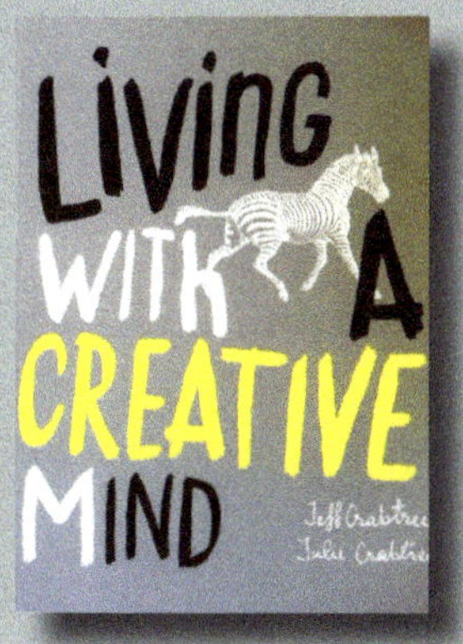

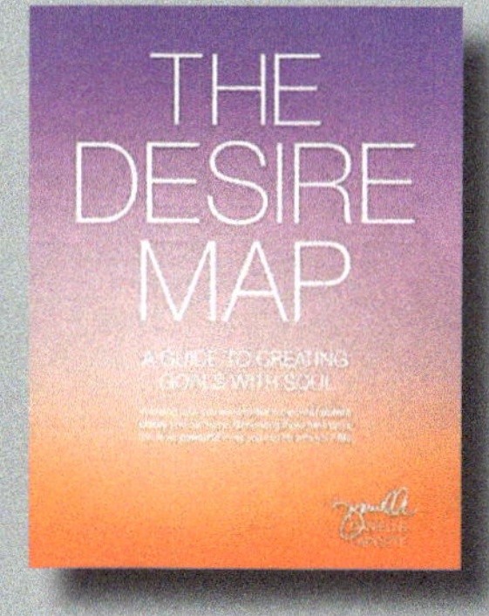

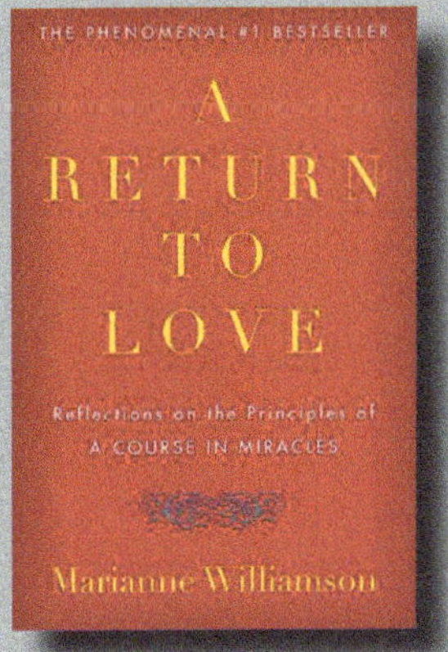

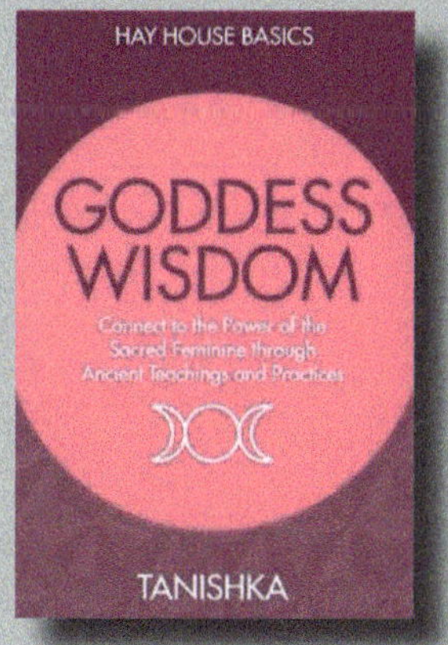

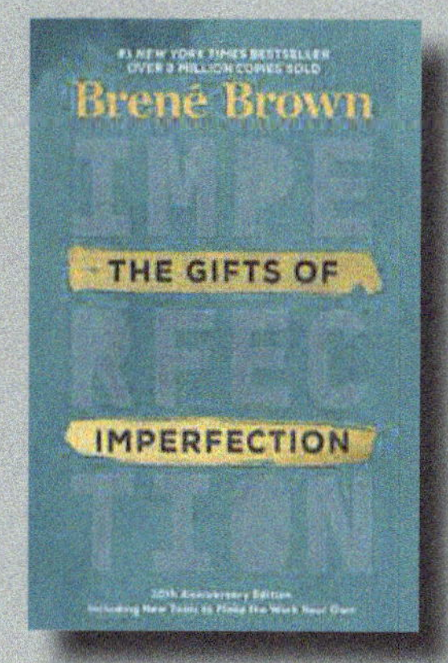

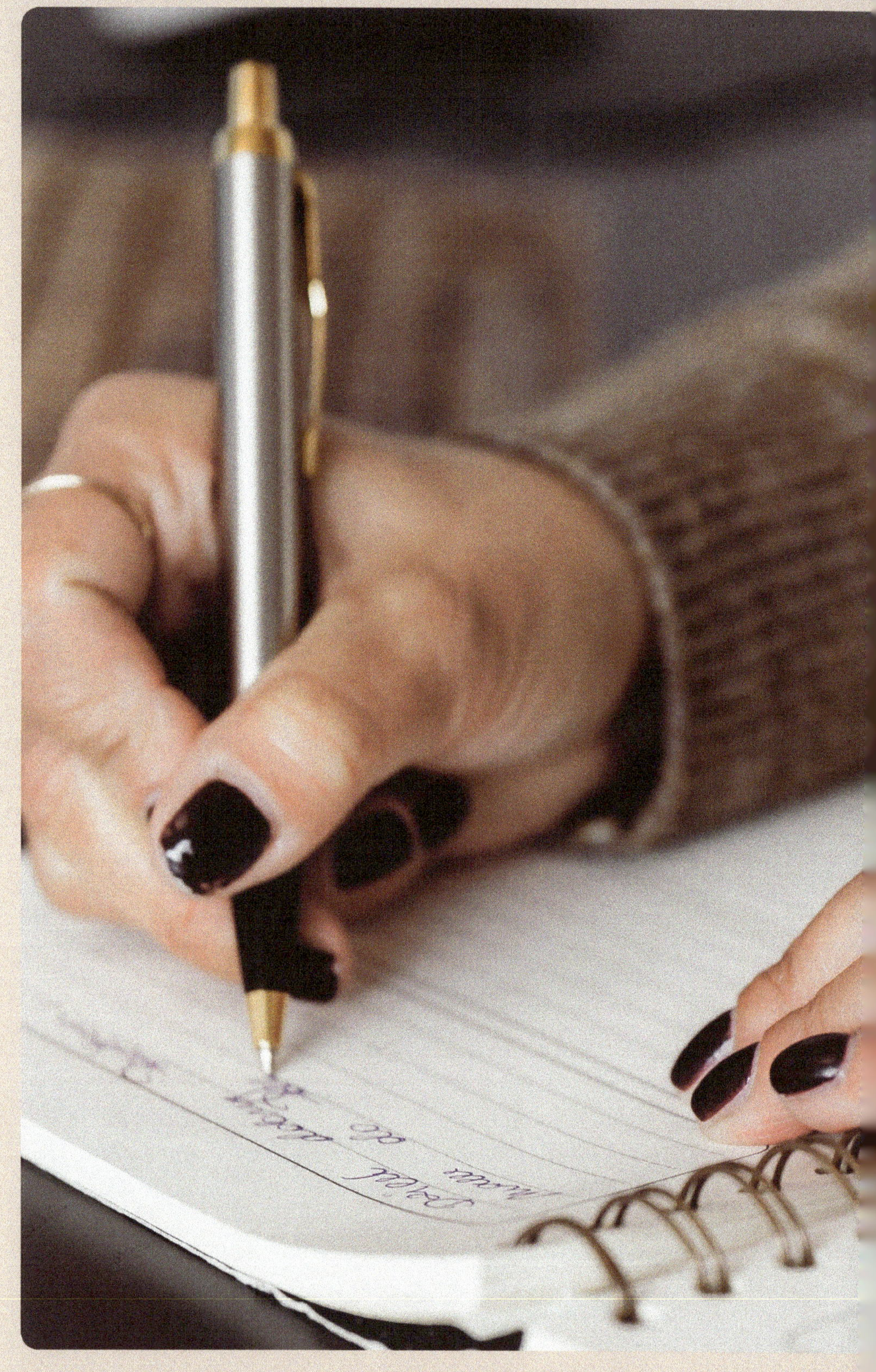

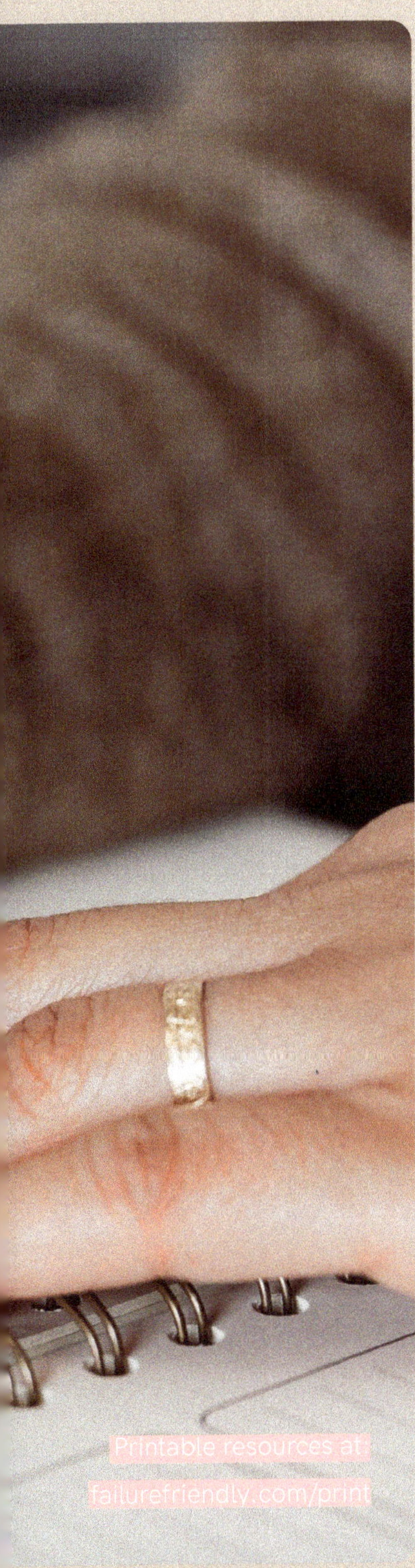

RESOURCES

The next section includes:

- Rules worksheet/poster
- Values worksheet/poster
- Warm up activities
- Learning activities
- Anxiety worksheet
- Confidence worksheet
- Face, Flip & Free worksheet
- Progress party worksheet
- Reframing guide
- Permission slip
- Body Scan worksheet
- Meditation guide
- The Process poster
- Triage Your Worries poster
- Notes

RULES

Everybody is accepted here

We use positive language

We seperate behaviour from identity

We go for quantity

We encourage wild ideas

We use constructive feedback

VALUES

Risk Taking

Friendliness

Openness

Curiosity

Play

Engagment

WARM UP ACTIVITIES

Breathing Exercise 4-4-4

Interrupt your thoughts by breathing in for 4 counts, holding the breath for 4, exhaling for 4 and again holding for 4 counts.

Speed Drawing

Complete a drawing from observation of the person next to you, your hand or anything in one minute - there is no time for fear!

Blind Drawing

Without looking at your page create a speedy blind drawing. This can also be done as an observation drawing without looking at your page - let the pencil follow your eye.

30 Circles

I'm going to give you a minute. On a sheet of paper with 30 circles you must adapt as many of those circle as you can into objects or drawings. For example you could turn one of them into a basketball, a face, turn two of them into a bicycle or three circles might make a traffic light.

Mr. Squiggle

A partner will draw squiggles on a page and you have one minute to turn those squiggles into a drawing of some sort.

List a many as you can

You will be given an everyday object such as a leaf or a paperclip and you are to brainstorm as many alternative uses for it as you can in one minute. Think outside the box!

Mission possible

What would a classroom without gravity look like? Imagine a world where tigers and butterflies could breed, the sky is the limit! Draw it or write a short story about it.

Rapid Dough

Without speaking with your partner or team, take turns to create a collaborative sculpture with thirty seconds building time each.

Upside-down Drawing

Complete a drawing from observation but draw it upside-down!

LEARNING ACTIVITIES

Ball Throwing / Talking Stick

Have a discussion, sharing ideas for a project or about an issue by throwing a ball or passing a talking stick. The goal is to share the ball (and the ideas) with as many people as possible in a short amount of time.

Thinking Tools

Sometimes to come up with ideas you need props, like a thinking hat for example. For ideas to come you need to stop thinking and use another part of your body, have a hoola hoop or some juggling balls in the class for students to use when they feel stuck.

Dress Ups

When presenting your ideas or research to the class, a class member or the teacher, it's fun to 'become' a reporter, artist, designer, art researcher or critic by getting into character with a costume! This can be a simple as a pair of glasses.

Playgrounds

Playtime doesn't need to stop at primary school, where possible schools should introduce playgrounds for secondary school students. These can include skate parks, roller skating rinks, trampolines, dance floors or rock climbing walls. All students should be consulted about the type activities they desire.

Music

Notice the way babies instinctively bop to music? It is human instinct to move to the beat. Music is a shortcut for loosening up, turning off the logical side of our brains just long enough to free our right creative side. Have students draw or work to music or have them express themselves with music

Animals

Animals bring out the playful side in all of us. Find ways for students to interact with animals in and out of the classroom.

ANXIETY

What does creative anxiety feel like?

Triggers

When does it happen?

Prevention

What can I do to prevent my triggers?

Commitment 1:

When I (insert your triggers) I will (insert your prevention methods).

Red Flags

What does it look like, what do I do in the early stage of creative anxiety?

Remedies

What can I do and how can I act to release stress when I feel anxious?

Commitment 2:

When I notice (insert your red flags) I will (insert your remedies).

CONFIDENCE

What does being confident feel like to me?

Positive cues

What makes me feel unstoppable?

Priming

What can I do to increase these cues?

Commitment 3:

I will (insert your priming practices) to give myself (insert your positive cues).

Sign Posts

What do I do when I feel confident in the creative process?

Habits & Rituals

What can I do regularly to encourage confident behaviour?

Commitment 4:

I will (insert your habits) daily/weekly to produce (insert sign posts behaviours).

FACE, FLIP & FREE

Face it

Finish this sentence honestly:
I feel anxious about…

Why?

Why?

Why?

Why?

Why?

Flip it

Flip your fear by reframing it into this statement:
I feel excited about…

Why?

Why?

Why?

Why?

Why?

Cheers fears!

Turn your previous fear into a positive affirmation by completing this sentence:
I am grateful for this fear because it's showing/teaching me that…

PROGRESS PARTY

Small steps make big impact

During the creative process it's easy to get overwhelmed by the ideas funnel (the mess you have to explore before you discover the great idea on the other side). Rather than having a pity party for yourself, direct your powerful brain to list all the work you've done that has led you to this point. Soon you will feel the momentum behind you, so ride it!

No step is too small! Start counting your achievements below.

For example, I have:

- *done my research*
- *scribbled some ideas*
- *tested ideas*
- *cleaned my desk*
- *eaten a healthy breakfast*
- *moved my body*
- *a similar task in the past*
- *talked it out with a friend*

REFRAMING GUIDE

Transform your thoughts to transform your life

This is a Mistake →	This is a Discovery
It's a disaster →	It's a process
I mucked up →	I learnt that...
It's wrong →	It's interesting because ...
I need to... / I have to... →	I can ...
I should... →	I'm allowed to ...
I can't... →	How can I?
I'm scared/nervous/anxious about... →	I'm excited about ...
I don't know about... →	I'm curious about ...
I'm not happy about... →	Wouldn't it be great if...
I'm struggling →	I'm learning that ...
I'm scared →	I'm ready
I don't have enough time →	Time is on my side
There's too much to do →	I have come so far, my life is so full
I don't know what to do →	I will know what to do when if feels right
I can't deal →	I enjoy the free fall
I don't have the answers →	Clarity comes from engagement.
I don't know where to start →	I have everything I need, such as ...
I don't know how to choose →	I choose to be calm, I choose to be confident
I don't know if I have what it takes →	I can do anything
This is proof that I'm not good enough →	This is proof that I'm daring and growing
I feel nervous →	I feel butterflies in my tummy
I want to give up →	I am being tested, I am getting stronger
I'm stressed/overwhelmed →	I need a break/ some me-time
I'm sick of this →	I can spice this up by...
What if it I fail? →	No matter what I will be alright
What will they think of me? →	I accept myself no matter what
I'm a fraud/an imposter →	I love learning new skills
I've already failed →	It's never too late
I've wasted so much time →	What is the smallest step I can take right now?
I don't know what to do →	I don't know what to do yet
I'm so worried →	I'm ready to back myself
This is hard →	This is living life outside of the comfort zone baby!
Who am I to do this? →	Why not me?
I just can't get started →	Why am I resisting?
The world is against me →	The universe supports me
This is going to be too hard →	This might be easier than I think, I can do hard things!
I might not have what it takes →	I've gotten through worse
There's so much to do →	I have come so far
I don't know what I'm doing →	I love challenges!
I've never done this before →	I am living my dreams
This is too big for me →	How can I break this down so it's manageable?
I am alone in this →	Who can I ask for help?
It's too risky →	Am I willing to fail in order to succeed?
It should to be perfect →	My best is enough
No-one has faith in me →	I have faith in me because...

PERMISSION SLIP

Expectations in check

There's a place for discipline and stretching towards excellence, but that place is not at the beginning of a new project. Rather than getting deterred at the first obstacle, let's set the tone for anti-perfectionism. By completing the permission slip below you can begin to embrace mistakes, befriend your doubt and smile at yourself as you figure it along the way!

PERMISSION SLIP

I,________________ , hereby declare that ________________

(Your Name) (Your Name)

has permission to be a clumsy student and make unlimited mistakes, take all the wrong turns and as many re-starts as possible, and ask lots of questions while I follow my curiosity and creativity.

Signed: ________________ Dated: ________________

(Your Signature)

BODY SCAN

- Your toes
- the souls of your feet
- your ankles
- your calves
- your shins
- your knees
- your thighs
- your hamstrings
- your hips
- your pelvis
- your belly
- your lower back
- your middle back
- your diaphragm
- your chest
- your heart
- your upper back
- your shoulders
- your biceps and triceps
- your elbows
- your forearms and wrists
- your hands
- your palms and fingers
- back of your hands
- your throat
- your neck
- your jaw
- your mouth
- your lips
- your tongue
- your teeth
- your nose and nostrils
- your cheeks
- your cheekbones
- your ears
- your earlobes
- your eardrums
- your eyelids
- your eyes
- your eyebrows
- your temples
- your third-eye
- your forehead
- crown of your head
- back of your head
- scan your whole body again

SELF COMPASSION

This is a guided meditation created by self compassion pioneer Kristen Neff. It is a variant on the classic Loving Kindness meditation practice, adjusted specifically to cultivate self compassion. You will need 10-20 minutes of uninterrupted time for this meditation.

- Get in a comfortable position, sitting upright and yet relaxed.
- Settle into your posture. Notice how your body feels, the sensation of your feet touching the floor, your bottom touching the seat. Be in your body right here right now, fully inhabiting your lived experience.
- Allow your attention to move outward to sounds. What sounds are arising outside your space? And then inside your space what do you hear?
- Now bring your focus to your breathing, inhaling and exhaling. Do you feel the breath most strongly at the nostrils, or in your chest as it rises and falls, or in the belly as it expands and releases? Take a few moments now to rest with our breath.
- Notice the peacefulness of resting and continue to breathe gently.
- Now bring to mind some aspect of your personality, a mistake you made or a failure that has been bothering you lately. Something that perhaps you've been criticising yourself for and has made you feel inadequate in some way. Whatever this trait or action is, try to get in touch with your feelings about it, how does it make you feel?

SELF COMPASSION

- See if you can locate the sensation, where are those emotions felt in the body? Allow them to be there instead of resisting these natural reactions that we feel when we judge ourselves. Ask yourself 'what am I feeling and where do I feel this in my body?'

- Get in touch with how much suffering is caused by our self judgment. Our fears of not being good enough. Some of our greatest suffering is caused by our own hands by a belief that we *should* be perfect.

- Take your hand, or both hands, and place it gently over your heart in a calm, soft, comforting manner. You may want to rub a reassuring circle. See if you can sense your heart right now. See if you can let your heart be moved by how difficult your emotional experience is, when you think about this thing that makes you feel bad about yourself.

- Repeat the following loving kindness phrases that are designed to help you feel compassion for the fact that you're an imperfect being, just like everyone else on this planet.

May I be safe.
May I be peaceful.
May I be kind to myself.
May I accept myself as I am.

SELF COMPASSION

- While feeling the warmth of your hand on your heart, repeat these phrases silently, trying to get in touch with the intention behind the words. The intention is to offer yourself kindness, compassion and acceptance. Giving yourself the same kindness and acceptance you would give to a good friend who was feeling bad about themselves.

- Repeat these phrases for five to fifteen minutes. When your mind wanders as it will inevitably do, just come back gently to the phrases.

- Remind yourself that everyone is in the same boat. Everyone feels inadequate in some way. We all fail and make mistakes. This is normal. This is something we all share. It's okay. Remembering all your fellow humans who also suffer from self judgement that way that you do, change the phrases slightly to include everyone in your intention for self compassion:

  May we all feel safe.
  May we all be peaceful.
  May we be kind to ourselves.
  May we accept ourselves as we are.

- Now see if you can feel what the compassionate self feels like. Maybe your heart feels warm or tingly. Notice the good qualities of an open heart, the feelings of care, kindness and connectedness.

- Lastly, thank yourself for being a good supportive friend.

THE PROCESS

1. IDEA STAGE / COMFORT ZONE
2. UNCERTAINTY / DISCOMFORT
3. MISTAKES / SELF DOUBT (GIVE UP?)
4. SURRENDER / ACCEPTANCE (GIVE IN!)
5. EXPERIMENT / PLAY
6. DISCOVERIES / HOPE
7. SATISFACTION / GROWTH
- EMOTIONS +
START > FINISH

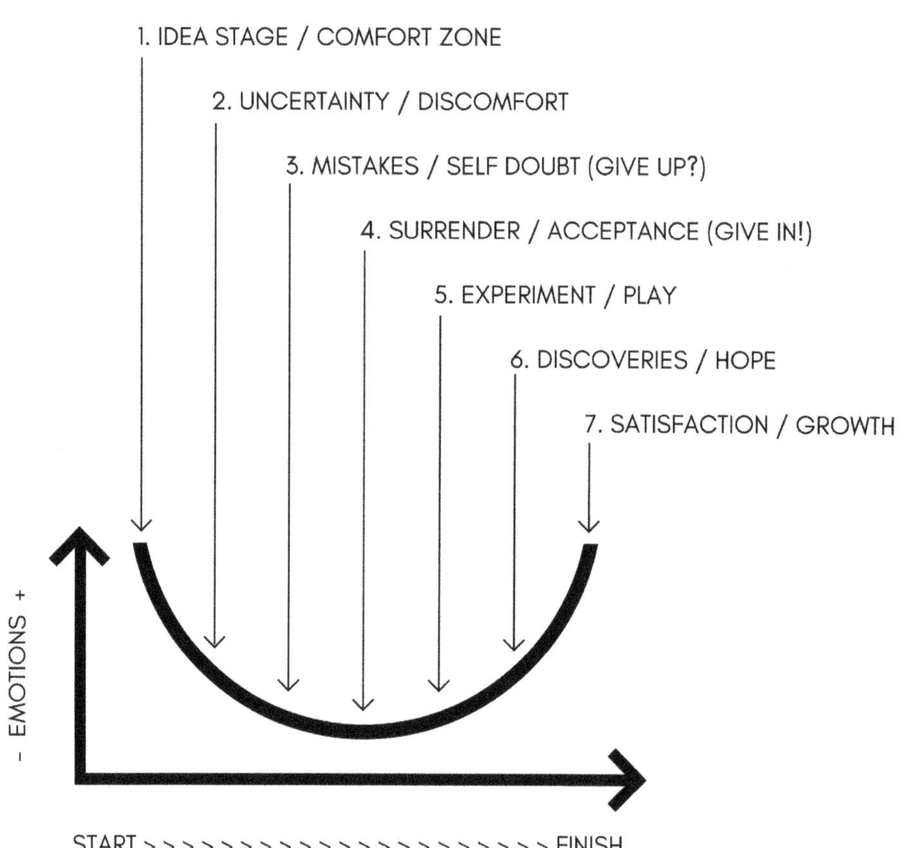

TRIAGE YOUR WORRIES

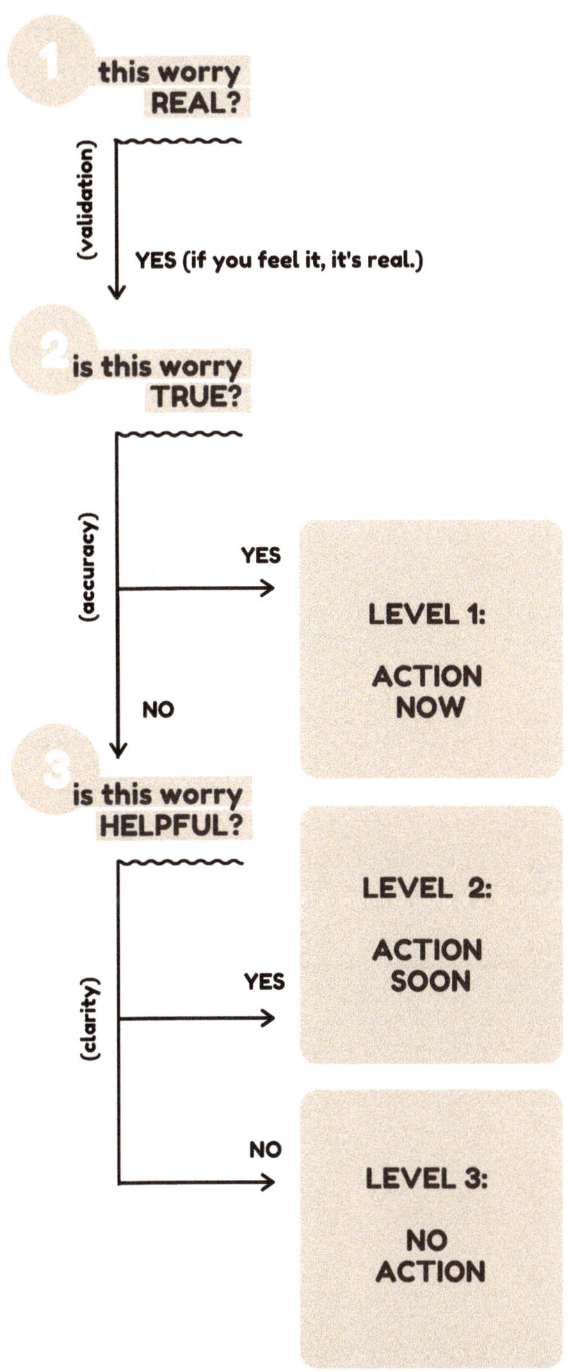

NOTES:

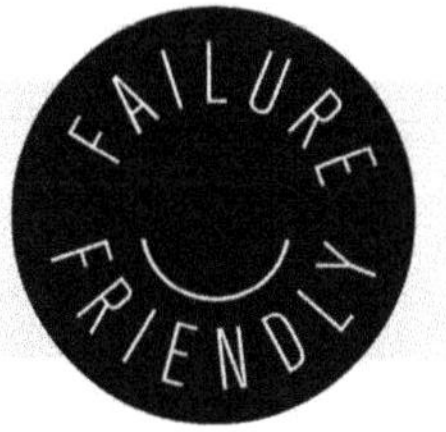
FAILURE
FRIENDLY

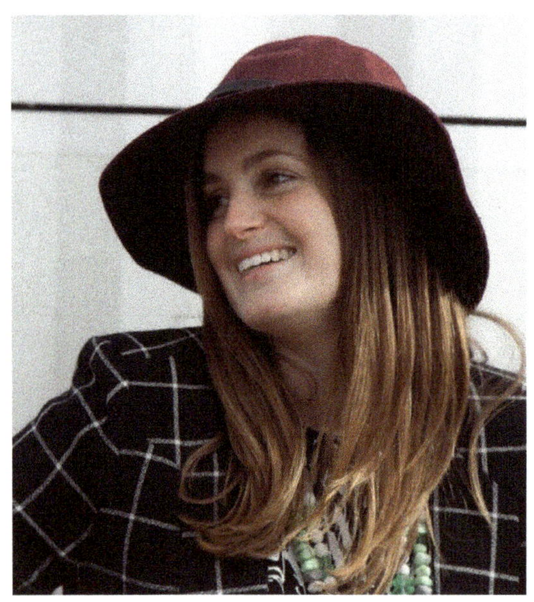

BUZZY LEWIS

Buzzy Lewis lives on Australia's Great Ocean Road, where the natural beauty inspires her endless creativity. Buzzy loves creativity. It lights her up, and it's how she pays the bills. She's been a graphic designer, marketing manager, artist, art teacher, entrepreneur and strategist.

But it's the dark side of creativity that she's obsessed with: creative anxiety, self-doubt and creative burnout. These slippery buggers have tormented her, sucked all of her energy and left her for dead, forcing her to look inside of herself, find resilience and grow into a better, stronger, calmer and more confident creative person.

It's this love-hate obsession with the dark side of creativity (and her desire to control it) that led Buzzy to stalk the mindsets of the world's most prolific creators and the work of scientists and researchers who have the answers. She's been smooshing these findings together nicely and neatly, like a true control freak, and sharing the results on her Failure Friendly blog since 2017.

The lockdown of 2020-2021 felt like the perfect time to reflect on everything this passion project had uncovered. A Word document of ideas quickly became the book you now hold in your hands. Buzzy said about the experience,

"Writing this book felt different to anything else I've created for Failure Friendly. For the first time I wasn't just writing for myself; I had a clear sense that it was for someone else: a creative person dreaming about a big life and exciting career but trapped in the smallness of their fear. Whoever you are, I hope this book finds you."

buzzy@failurefriendly.com

failure_friendly

failurefriendly

www.ingramcontent.com/pod-product-compliance
Ingram Content Group UK Ltd.
Pitfield, Milton Keynes, MK11 3LW, UK
UKHW062313290726
14090UKWH00018B/1047